Road Dirt

The Musings & Ramblings

Of A Biker Preacher

Rob Brooks

ISBN: 1492360104
ISBN-13: 978-1492360100

DEDICATION

This book is dedicated to my mother and father.
Their encouragement and example continue to inspire me.

CONTENTS

ACKNOWLEDGMENTS

My wife Lisa has put up with my many hours of writing, compiling, and editing these pages. Her support and encouragement in my meandering life, as well as during this process, is something I can never fully repay her for.
I am most thankful for my Lord and Savior Jesus Christ, who has given me life, new life, and the experiences contained in these pages. These pages, this life, would not exist without Him.

(cover photo by Jeff McPhail)

1 IN MY BLOOD

Motorcycles are in my blood, in my DNA. I've seen them under a microscope, floating in my blood stream, riding the highways and byways of my veins and arteries. Microscopic sport bikes, cruisers, old classics, inherited from my mother and father, racing through my circulatory system, dodging in and out of the red cell traffic, avoiding the white cell cops.

I was born to ride.

Okay, so "in my blood" may be a bit of a stretch, but I did come from a motorcycle riding family, and riding is one of my great passions, my favorite pastime. My father was a rider back in his youth, a "greaser" in the late 50s, riding a '54 Triumph Tiger 500 with my mom hanging on for dear life. The original "Fonz." (They still ride, by the way- both in their 70s) The bike had chopped fenders, a chrome frame, removable baffles, and a pink peanut tank. He sold that bike before joining the Air Force, and no photos remain of it. Pity. He even rode while stationed on the island of Okinawa, hopping up Cushmans and running aviation fuel in them, blasting along rough roads between the base and local villages and towns.

As children, my brothers and I saw various bikes come and go in Dad's workshop- a '67 Triumph TR6, a '68 Bonneville, and enough extra parts hanging from pegs on the walls to practically build another. We rode minibikes, dirt bikes, cut miles of trails through the woods behind our north Georgia home. We even got to ride his Triumph up and down the street when we were old enough, under Dad's watchful, and Mom's worried, eyes. Hunting, fishing, camping, riding- it was the ideal boyhood.

Once I got my driver's license, I bought my first car, a '73 Ford Pinto, and left behind two wheels for four. Girls, cruising, graduation, college, grad school, marriage, ministry, children- motorcycling became a faded memory, fond recollections from a storied childhood.

Then in 1996, it happened. Driving home one afternoon from the church I served at, I saw a shiny black and chrome Honda V65 Magna at the end of a driveway, with a "FOR SALE" sign on it. Something deep, old, awakened inside me. I pulled over to gawk at this pristine piece of art on two wheels. It was beautiful. I was hooked. I drove by it every day for a week, slowing down, lingering over it, devising ways to come up with the cash to buy it, but more important, how to talk my wife into letting me buy it. Then one day it was gone, but the beast had been reawakened in me. I wanted to ride again, I had to ride again.

After some clever, persuasive appeals (translate: incessant begging & groveling), Lisa reluctantly gave the "green light", and my quest began. I wisely enrolled in an MSF beginner riding course, searched the classifieds for weeks, and finally found a blue

'93 Suzuki VS800 Intruder. I purchased the bike, took the MSF experienced rider course on it, and began to feed the need. I discovered some other guys in the church that rode, joined a local CMA chapter, rode to a couple of "Bike Weeks", and generally immersed myself in the world of motorcycling. I loved riding, enjoyed the freedom of the open road, found many opportunities to make new friends, enjoy God, and share my faith with others while riding my motorbike.

But as can sometimes happen with even a good thing, my life got a little unbalanced. While still very involved with my family activities and duties, I had begun to spend too much of my free time riding, leaving my wife and our girls behind. Lisa began to resent my motorcycle riding, but kept her feelings to herself. I of course, was completely oblivious, thinking everything was right with my little world.

I took a position at a different church in January of 2000, just two towns over. Riding home one afternoon in April, a left-turner at a stop sign thought he found a gap in north-bound traffic, and jumped out. Instead, he found me. Two broken-up legs, four surgeries, and six months at the hands of "physical terrorists" left me wondering if I would ever walk right again, much less ride again. Yet on the one-year anniversary of my accident, I borrowed a bike from a friend at church, and with another biker from church, spent the day "getting back in the saddle" so to speak. Unbeknownst to my wife, who upon finding out was none too happy with neither me nor my "partners in crime."

Sensing the inevitable though, Lisa eventually gave in to my desire to ride again, declaring, "I've got a fat insurance policy on you now, so if you get yourself killed, I'll grieve, but I'm moving to Tahiti." Gotta love that woman! A fellow rider at my church knew a Yamaha Motors executive that was selling his motorcycle, a 1998 Royal Star Tour Classic. It had been a company bike given to him, and he racked up about 5100 miles on it, slathered it in over $3000 worth of chrome and accessories...then garaged it and bought a Harley! All his riding buddies rode Harleys, so he was selling the Royal Star. Imagine that- a Yamaha executive ditching the company bike to ride the competition. Priceless.

He heard my story, called me on the phone one afternoon, and shocked me when he stated, "I'll let you have the bike for what I got in it." Wow! I called my wife, exclaiming, "I found it! My new bike! Call the bank..." And the rest, as they say, is history. Over 10 years, 77,000 miles, and countless roads later, I'm still riding that old Royal Star, and even own a sport bike now, a '99 Triumph Sprint ST. The people I've met, the places I've been, the memories I've made, the opportunities to experience Christ and share Him with others out on the open road, have filled my cup to overflowing. And continues to, but with a better balance and perspective this time. My girls love to ride with me, my wife, not yet, but I'm working on her! I think my story may contain some elements you can relate to, may even mirror parts of your story as well. My prayer is that the entries in this book will encourage you along your journey, hopefully even help you grow closer to "the Lord of the open road", and find Christ to be your ultimate "Road Captain."

The book chronicles my reflections, observations, and meditations on riding and life. The stories herein are compiled from my notes, journals, and blog entries over the past eight to ten years. They are grouped topically into chapters, and are chronological within that form. May my blessings and life lessons become yours as well.

Let's take a little ride together...

2 ROAD TRIPS

Friday, Oct. 2, 2009

I returned home last night from a 4-day road trip with my dad & mom. This was the first time we brought mom along, and the 3 of us had a great time riding the roads of NE Alabama. I rode down Monday morning to their lake house, where we loaded up the bikes in their "toy-hauler" and headed west for Alabama. It took most of the day to finally arrive at Desoto State Park on Lookout Mtn. We set up camp, built a fire, and planned out the next day's ride.

Tuesday morning arrived cool and clear, but I awoke with an upset stomach, so we delayed our departure until about noon. I finally felt good enough to ride, so we pulled out and rode down to Desoto Falls. These falls are spectacular! A 3-tiered falls, that finally plunges over 100 ft into its own canyon, we stood in awe of the majesty of the roaring waters. Standing near the edge and looking over was almost dizzying- the roar of the waters, the depth of the gorge, the sheer cliffs carved out by the power of water- it was an amazing moment. We rode on over to Little River Falls and Canyon next. These falls were not as high as Desoto Falls, but still over 45 ft high, and wider. We were able to walk around near the edge, but careful not to step too close to the edges. Funny, we saw signs at both places saying, "Jumping Prohibited from the Falls." I'm sure there have been idiots who tried it anyway! The sound of rushing waters and the roar of the falls called to mind the verse in the Bible that describes the voice of God as that of "the sound of many waters." My mother could have stayed there all day, soaking in the sound of the falls. After riding some more beautiful mountain roads, we made our way back to the campsite for supper and sitting by the campfire, under a bright moon. Perfect ending to day 1.

Wednesday we saddled up and rode down into the valley to the town of Ft. Payne. This is the home of the legendary country super-group Alabama, and there are memorials to them everywhere. We visited the Ft Payne Train Depot & Museum, the Opera House, several noteworthy stores and cafe's, and took pictures with larger-than-life statues of the band at the Alabama Memorial in the middle of town. What a great little town! Lots of inspiration there for country music, for sure.

We then rode back up the mountain and hopped on the Lookout Mtn. Parkway, and rode it along the ridge all the way down to Gadsden. There we found the Noccalula Falls & Gorge. This waterfall drops 90 ft. into the Black Creek ravine, where water has carved out a fascinating deeply-rounded cavern underneath. We then visited the Gadsden-Etowah County War Memorial, with tributes to those who gave their lives from that region from WW I to Gulf War I. It was a small but fitting tribute. We saddled up and rode back up the Parkway to Desoto, and again enjoyed supper by a warm campfire under a rising bright moon. Ahh, soothes the soul.

Thursday brought a change of plans. We had planned to stay an extra day and ride Thursday over to Cloudland Canyon, and return home Friday, but something told me to examine my rear tire. A look revealed a shock- the tread had nearly worn completely down all along the center, and in one spot the tread had worn smooth. I couldn't believe it! I knew the tire was getting worn, but I thought I could make it through this trip before replacing it. That was not to be. Rather than risking another 100-200 miles on it in another state, we sadly broke camp and loaded everything up for the long trip home. It was a beautiful drive, heading SE out of the Alabama mountains & hill country, back into sunny GA. I kept thinking about how I'd love to be riding this home on my bike, rather than in my mom & dad's truck. They reminded me of what I really already knew- God is in control, and who knows but that He might have saved us from a situation that could have been anywhere from inconvenient to catastrophic.

I actually did get to finish the trip on my bike, however. We drove to Oxford, GA where we unloaded my bike for the ride home, and my parents turned south toward their lake house. I rode back home under a nearly full moon over my right shoulder, praising God for the great sights & memories of our trip together. There will be other trips, I am hopeful.

Tomorrow- a new tire!

*The following is the day-by-day account of an epic cross-country excursion I made in 2010 with my good friend Mike Hinton. It contains information I had journaled nightly while on the trip, when the day's events were still fresh in my mind. I hope you can imagine yourself riding with us!

ROAD TRIP 2010

Mike & Rob's Excellent Adventure!

Saturday, September 18

I awoke at 6:45am, after a restless night of partial sleep, anticipating getting on the road. Mike and I both have been excited yet a little nervous- neither of us had ever been on the road trip this far out and for as long as we were going on this one. With the bike loaded, I geared up, woke Lisa and the girls to say my early morning goodbyes. After many hugs and kisses, I pulled out for Mike's house. After he did the same, we got on the road about 8:45am. We negotiated traffic south on I-85, west around North Atlanta on I-285, then north on I-75 to Chattanooga, Tennessee. I had been a little anxious about riding on interstates around the metro area, but once on the open road, we settled into a good 65-70 mph pace.

We took I-24 west out of Chattanooga, and stopped for lunch at a Cracker Barrel outside town. I spent a year of my life in this city after I graduated from high school, at Precept Ministries. I fell in love with this "city in a valley" back then, with the Tennessee River flowing through it, and riding through brought back memories of living here, exploring the sights, attractions, and the countryside. We rode hard all the way to Nashville, 137 miles. We skirted south of town, and swung true west for the first time, pointing the bikes toward Memphis on I-40. We chased the sun across the sky for the 200 miles it took, stopping a few times for rest and fuel. We passed through Memphis with a setting sun in our eyes, and as we exited the city, the Mississippi River Bridge and the Arkansas state line were back dropped by a bright orange and red sunset. Beautiful.

We pulled into a KOA campsite just after dark, in Marion, Arkansas, just over the river. A little shameless commercial- KOAs are incredible! At least this one was. A tent site, with power and water, for $10 per tent, with Mike's KOA rewards card. Great deal. We set up, then I showered and texted/called my family back home and a few friends who wanted daily updates. I decided to stay up and read some before turning in, and made the mistake of leaving the tent flap open while I sat on a picnic bench outside. By the time I hopped in the bedroll, I noticed the tent was full of mosquitoes! I must have spent the next hour slapping and swatting bugs, and I'm sure Mike heard me. Note to self: never leave your tent open, for even a minute, while tent-camping along the shores of the "Mighty Mississippi."

Today- Georgia and Tennessee. Tomorrow- Arkansas and Oklahoma!

Sunday, September 19

We packed up early and pulled out of Marion, running west on I-40. East Central Arkansas is the most desolate countryside to ride I have ever done so far. Miles and hours of endless farmland, or forests, right up the highway, and all straight, all flat. It got nerve-wracking at times, with precious few towns and turnoffs for gas stops! We finally made it to Little Rock after lunch, having been cooked in temperatures approaching 100 degrees by mid-day. We stopped at a KFC, then rode on toward Ft. Smith. I must say, the western part of this state was just the opposite- beautiful, scenic, with hills, towns, sweeping highways, and splendid sights. Mucho better!

We finally crossed into the great state of Oklahoma! Officially now in the west. We stopped at a welcome center, which was closed (nice to know there are still some places closed on Sundays), but met a burly, dark-skinned, tattooed Harley rider who pulled in right after us, with a long braided ponytail and braided beard to match. He was from the state, returning home from riding up and down the east coast, Maine to Florida, alone. Wow, we are novices compared to him. He gave us some tips for great places to stop in Oklahoma, and we saddled up and decided to try and make for Oklahoma City by nightfall, halfway across the state. As we rode on, suddenly a drop of sunscreen lotion, which I had been applying at nearly every stop, mixed with sweat on my brow, and sank into my left eye. Instantly, my eye felt like it was on fire, and literally gushed with tears. Barely able to see, big tractor-trailer rigs and general traffic all around, I got to the side of the road, yanked my helmet off, and began dousing my eyeball with my water bottle. Mike, who had been ahead of me, somehow doubled back when he discovered I was no longer behind him, and found me beside the road bottoms-up with the water bottle over my eye. After a few minutes, the pain faded, I put in some eye drops for the redness, and we were on our way. Whew, that was painful!

Night began to fall, and we were still not quite in Oklahoma City. We stopped for fuel, fluids, and to don our night riding reflector vests over our jackets. We shot through the city after dark, and proceeded on to El Reno, 45 miles to the west. Monotonous, long stretches of blacktop, into the night, to get there. We finally pulled into the El Reno West KOA at 9:45pm, local time. Tired, hungry, sore, we cleaned up, threw out sleeping bags in the bunks of a cabin we had booked, and sank into deep sleep. Two very long days, both miles and hours in the saddle, nearly 500 miles each.

Monday, September 20

We packed up our bikes after a restful night's sleep in the cabin, and hopped back on I-40 West. Almost immediately, we found ourselves riding against a hard, south to north wind blowing against our left at 25-35mph. The hard winds continued all day, blowing us all over our lane, especially when we encountered large trucks. The air turbulence around the trucks, combined with the strong winds, beat us mercilessly. Exhausting. We took frequent stops, as much to rest as to see the sights.

And what sights there were to see! The rolling hills of Oklahoma and North Texas prairie lands were a sight to behold. As we rode, I imagined these lands flowing with buffalo herds, as far as the eye could see. We saw huge, energy windmills, both sides of the interstate. We found "The Mother Road", old Route 66, and spent some time off the interstate, riding this fabled piece of Americana. We visited the National Route 66 Museum in Elk City, Oklahoma, and spent a couple of hours in this fascinating indoor and outdoor exhibit. We had no idea this place existed, until we saw a roadside billboard for it. Still on 66, we rode through Weatherford, Oklahoma, where we actually found our first "66" intersection sign.

After crossing into north Texas, the state of my birth, we came upon the town of McLean, a town once booming with life, but virtually dead after I-40 came through, bypassing the old Route 66. Its interesting to me, how some towns reinvented themselves when the interstate replaced 66, and continue to thrive, while others like McLean rolled up the welcome mat and have slowly faded away. Sad. We did find a national marker in McLean, the original "Phillips 66" station in Texas, rebuilt by the side of the road, replete with original fuel pumps, still showing leaded gas for .19 per gallon. That was a cool photo op, for sure.

Eventually, the rolling prairie gave way to the elevated plains and flatlands on the Texas Panhandle, and massive ranches as far as one could see. Still leaning into strong northward winds against us, we rolled into legendary Amarillo! Looking up the local KOA east of town, we found their prices were too steep, for cabins or tent sites. Would have been tough to set up tents in the wind anyway. Besides, the campground was next to an Air Force base, and backed up to a railroad track. Too pricey, too windy, too noisy. No way. We settled upon a local Sleep Inn, which Mike had a discount card for. This guy is great to travel with! After checking ourselves in, as we began to unload our gear, we met in the parking lot a Gold Wing rider from Rhode Island, riding solo all the way to San Francisco. He called himself "Chick." Cool. We walked across the parking lot to a Cracker Barrel (these are everywhere!), got a bite, then hit a Harley shop next to it, to just walk and gawk. Oh, and buy the customary t-shirt.

Across the rest of Oklahoma, and into the Panhandle of Texas, Route 66 much of the way, with scenic small towns and sights, this was a 240-mile day. With the winds, it felt like 500! Whew, what a day.

Tuesday, September 21

How do I begin to describe this day? Just the most amazing day
yet of this trip. We checked out of the hotel and rode over to the
local Texas Information Center. They directed us to our day's
destinations.

First stop, Palo Duro Canyon State Park. We rode south of
Amarillo about 35 miles, across the flattest land I have ever seen.
Suddenly, the scenery changed, and we were in sagebrush and
canyonlands. We entered this state park, the second largest
canyon in the country, behind Grand Canyon. I could not believe I
had never heard of this place. Beautiful beyond description.
Unlike Grand, there is a paved road that winds and descends to
the canyon floor, and runs the length of the park. We rode it,
stopping at various places to take photos, hike, climb, and just
drink it all in, slack-jawed. It was like walking and riding through
scenes from some old Clint Eastwood western. We could have
stayed there for days- literally! There are campsites throughout
the basin of the canyon. Something I was informed of at a
welcome center- this valley and its history was part of the
inspiration behind the television miniseries "Lonesome Dove"
back in 1985. What a stark, barren, beautiful place.

Next, we rode back up into Amarillo to the famous Big Texan
Steakhouse, home of the 72 oz Steak Challenge. As the story goes,
if you can finish off their massive steak, and all side dishes, within
one hour, your whole meal is free, and you enter their record
books. Many have tried, few have succeeded. We didn't even try.
But the food and atmosphere was fantastic!

We then rode out to the popular "Cadillac Ranch" west of town,
which is ten old Caddies buried nose-deep in the ground, single

file. Everyone who walks through it has the opportunity to "leave your mark" with a can of spray paint. We sprayed our names on the left fender of one, took some pics, and rode on. Ok, been there, done that.

We had been told of a place known as the Midpoint Café in Adrian, Texas. It is at the exact midpoint of the old Route 66. We found, it, still on a drivable portion of the famed road, and decided to pull in, exactly as two other motorcyclists did, followed by a senior couple in a pickup truck with a camper on it. They had just closed, but as we looked in, the two ladies who operate it suddenly came to the door and welcomed us in, reopening just for us six wayward travelers! They served us up some fresh-squeezed, ice-cold orange juice, and a helping of their "World Famous Ugly Crust Pie." We stayed there nearly an hour, chatting with the two sweet proprietors Fran and Joann, the camper couple, and the two riders. They each had fascinating stories of their own. One of the riders, an elderly gent on a Suzuki V-Strom named Alan, was from "across the pond" in England! He had shipped his bike over to New York City, and had been riding America for a month. He was headed to the Grand Canyon, and had just picked up his traveling companion Rick in Amarillo, who himself was riding his Gold Wing from Toronto, Canada, doing the same thing- riding across America. They both were well up in their 60s, full of youthful enthusiasm and energy. The camper couple was from Massachusetts, the state my parents are both from, driving to San Francisco to meet up with their son, who planned to give his father a motorcycle ride across the San Fran Bridge! The Midpoint Café, we learned, was the inspiration for "Flo's V-8 Café" in the Disney Pixar cartoon "Cars", and its easy to see why. Inside and out, the café is decorated with nostalgia from the glory days of the Mother Road. We wrote our names on their "Graffiti Truck" in the parking lot, purchased a few souvenirs in the small gift shop, and after saying our goodbyes and exchanging emails all around, Mike and I rode on westward.

Leaving the Texas high plains for the mesas of the old west, we crossed into New Mexico at sunset. We rode on to the town of Tucumcari, with a glorious sunset directly before us, setting over the buttes and mesas in the distance, and a bright full moon directly behind us. The colors in the sky faded from bright gold, to orange, then red out front, to purple, blue, and finally black out back. It was an amazing moment in time, riding in that. An eternity was wrapped up in those moments as we descended into Tucumcari. We pulled into the KOA outside of town, up on a small hill, checked in and set up our tents in a steadily increasing wind.

Mike had quipped before we left on our trip: "You know, even better than the places we'll visit, will be the people we'll meet." I had tucked that thought away, and it certainly was proving to be true. More than the amazing sights and places we visited today, the best part really had been the people we encountered. There was the young lady we met back at Palo Duro, travelling alone across America from Rhode Island to California; Sarah, our waitress at the Big Texan, who was actually a single mom from Missouri, looking for a new life out west; Fran and Joann at Midpoint Café, the sweetest ladies in Texas; the old riders, Rick and Alan, new-found friends on the road; Fred from Phoenix, Arizona, heading east for Vermont, living out of his SUV with two Rottweilers, two Dobermans, and a German Shepherd! Each person had their own unique story, and each have enriched the journey for us both, as much if not more than the places we've visited. I prayed for each of them by name before turning in for a tent camp under a full moon.

Texas and New Mexico- many memories, many miles. More tomorrow.

It's gonna be a blustery night...

Wednesday, September 22

After a breezy night under a bright moon, we awoke to a cloudy, drizzly, windy and noticeably cooler morning. It went downhill from there. We ate breakfast, bought some bottled waters and ice, then loaded up to continue west. We rode old Route 66 through downtown Tucumcari, once a booming, gleaming city along the Mother Road, now mostly run down. Old neon signs dotted the street, vestiges of a bygone era.

About eight miles west of town on I-40, I realized my wallet was not in my jacket's inner pocket. We pulled over, and took apart both bikes by the side of the road, frantically searching for it. We rode back, with me in a near panic. All of my cash, cards, identification, medical info, etc. in that billfold. We split up, Mike riding back through Tucumcari to search along the sides of the street we came down, while I bee-lined back to the KOA campground. I had the entire KOA staff helping me comb the place- the office, our tent site, the parking areas, bathrooms, TV/game room, even the trash cans. Nothing. We scoured the frontage road leading into and out of the KOA site, two to three times, to no avail. Depressed, I called Lisa back home in Georgia, had her cancel all the cards, left our contact info with the KOA manager, then prepared to ride into town to fill out a police report and find a way to get some money wired to me. Turning onto the frontage road, there not 100 yards up on the right side, was my wallet! We had walked by that spot three times, and now there it was. Someone had it all along, and tossed it there in between searches. All of my cash, cards, and a gas gift card were missing, yet incredibly, my IDs and medical cards were present. Strange. We rode back to the KOA office, to tell them. We and the manager came to suspect one of their employees, Phil, who had coincidentally drove into town on "errands" earlier, but since no one saw anything, it was hard to accuse. We rode into town to the police station, made out a report, and an officer said he would question the "suspect" later that day and contact me if they turned up anything. I wasn't holding my breath.

Having done all we could, having left our contact info everywhere, we deliberated what to do. Calling home, Lisa said to ride on, she could wire money to a Western Union in town. Yet as we sat at a local Burger King (which Mike had to spring for), we overheard a weather alert warning of massive storms with heavy rains, strong winds, and dangerous flooding, all across Arizona and rapidly moving east, our way. Our mind was made up for us. We decided to turn around, and make hard for Amarillo. Plans change with circumstances.

The winds howled against us all the way back, south to north, on our right side this time. We rode through several small rain showers before arriving back in Amarillo, staying at the same Sleep Inn as before, Mike covering the cost. He said, "Don't worry about figuring out how to get cash wired out. I'll get us both, and we can settle up later." A good friend. That night back in the hotel, we decided to change course and run south to Wichita Falls and on to Dallas, to my brother Rick's place, who had said we could ride out the coming storms with them. Sounded like a plan.

Looking back, God may have actually protected us from bigger calamity than a stolen wallet. The next two days saw intense storms and floods across Arizona and New Mexico, with several deaths reported. We could have never crossed under those conditions. I also retained my identification, insurance, and medical info, which was a blessing. God is good- things could have been much worse for us, on both counts.

Hey, we'll make new memories and meet new people all the way home, by an entirely different route. This could still be great fun! "Excellent Adventure, Part 2".

Thursday, September 23

We woke up, packed up, filled up, and rolled out of Amarillo in a windy, cold, rainy morning. We said our goodbyes to Route 66 and set off southwest on Hwy. 287 toward Wichita Falls. We slogged through heavy rain and driving winds for almost an hour and a half, trying to outrun the storms chasing us from the west. The road was mostly deserted save the occasional semi truck, and in some places our pace slowed to 25-35mph, with water in these flat lands up to our floorboards at times. Scary riding in these conditions. We dared not stop for long in the small towns that dotted our route along the way, eager to make south Dallas and my brother Rick's house by nightfall.

Finally, after what seemed like an eternity of wet, wind, and exhaustion, the weather began to break. We were outrunning the storms. Before long, we rode off the Panhandle's high plains, and into the northeast Texas rolling hills and prairie lands. Despite the remaining, lingering rain, we found this to be beautiful country. We rumbled through numerous small Texas towns, each with their own flavor and Lone Star pride: Clarendon, Estelline, Childress, Quanah, Vernon, to name a few. The further southeast we rode, the more distance we put between us and the storm front we had ridden (almost swam) through. By the time we hit

Wichita Falls, the skies had cleared, the temps had climbed, and our spirits had lifted. After a brief pause in town, we continued south down 287, and the prairie gave way to farm land, then rolling hills of cottonwood. We even rode through vast oil fields between the towns of Henrietta and Bowie! Miles of rigs, bobbing up and down under the Texas sun. We rode along a ridgeline overlooking the valley of Springtown and North FT. Worth. After battling the stifling traffic of Ft. Worth, we finally rolled into Rick & Robyn's place in Mansfield around 7:45pm. Rick took Mike and I out for a bite at a local barbeque joint, then we spent the evening in their living room, recounting our experiences of the last six days. After calling Lisa and the girls back home, exchanging some e-correspondence and loading some photos up on Facebook, we called it a night.

Again, we met some wonderful people today- the young mother in Childress who offered to top off our gas tanks; the old man with the huge cross around his neck, who warned us of bad weather to our south, and then prayed over us; the black lady in Mansfield who very compassionately pulled up alongside me at an off ramp to inform me, "Sir, you're in the wrong lane. Here, pull up in front of me." Like Tuesday, a memorable day of riding, although nerve-wracking and exhausting, and kind folks all along the way.

A note: Somewhere north of Ft. Worth, my Royal Star odometer passed 50,000 miles. May it carry me another 50K.

Friday, September 24

Mike and I spent the day resting and recharging at Rick's place in Mansfield. We slept in, read, watched TV, played with their dogs out back, and just hung out with the family as they came home. We needed this today.

We went out to eat at a quirky little restaurant this evening called "Freebirds." Similar to a Moes back home, but way funkier. There is a stretched chopper hanging from the ceiling, straddled by "Lady Liberty". Too cool. We chowed on king-size burritos, and piles of fresh chips.

Its been great to see my brother, sis-in-law, nephew and niece. Tomorrow, on to Mike's sister's house!

Saturday, September 25

We awoke to heavy rain showers all across the Dallas-Ft. Worth metroplex. Flash flood warnings were being broadcast citywide, so Mike and I weren't leaving anytime soon. We ate, talked, played cards and video games, and of course, watched football. The weather looked it might break sometime mid-afternoon, so Rick suggested we all go for a bite at a local Cracker Barrel. Finally by about 2:00pm, the rain ceased. Mike and I packed the bikes, suited up, said our goodbyes to Rick, Robyn, and the kids, and took off east on I-20.

It's been said that Dallas is where the east begins, and Ft. Worth is where the west begins. So, we finally said goodbye to the west, entering the east Texas piney forests. Like the previous east-bound days, we eventually outran the storms, and rode in the fading sunlight. By 7:00pm, we rolled into Gary, Texas, and Mike's sister's place.

I love Debbie and Ronnie's homestead! The house is an old converted train station that had been moved to the 12-acre property, with a stocked pond and two motorcycles in the barn out back, a Harley and a BMW. I like these folks already. They had a carnivore's delight cooked up for us when we unloaded: fire-cooked hotdogs, huge hamburgers, and barbeque ribs. I am not going to sleep well tonight, but delicious doesn't even come close. The evening ended with all four of us watching the original "Jaws" movie on their big screen. Ahh, memories from my childhood. Or should I say nightmares? Off to bed.

Sunday, September 26

We awoke to the smell of bacon and biscuits that Debbie was cooking up for us, then I prepared to call in to talk live with the children of the RockiTown children's church hours back at Hebron! At exactly 10am and 11:30am Eastern Time, Jeff called my cell phone, having plugged his into the sound system in the worship room. Both times, I could hear the cheering and screaming of 100+ kids as my voice rang out over their room speakers. I recounted the trip highlights, and the kids were wowed by the places Mike and I had been, and the things we had seen and experienced. What a thrill to call back home, and share the trip with over 200 kids and leaders at once!

After lunch, we loaded up our gear, said our goodbyes to Mike's kin, and rolled out. I thoroughly enjoyed our time with Debbie and Ronnie- old biker folks themselves, having ridden all over north America, the four corners of our great land. We rode up and back out of Texas for the last time after a total of 7 days in and out of the state.

We rode back to I-20 in Shreveport, Louisiana, and tried to cross the state as fast as possible. Three statements best describe our view of north Louisiana- flat, woods, lousy roads. We couldn't get across the Mississippi River fast enough. We finally crossed the great river and got into Mississippi around 6pm. At a gas station across the river, we deliberated whether or not we should continue on to Meridian to a KOA campground there, or find a hotel nearby for the night and visit the Vicksburg Civil War museum in the morning. After considering riding through Jackson in rush hour traffic, a band of bikers pulled up to us in the parking lot, wearing the patches of the Banditos outlaw club. They pulled up close to us, looked us over, and one of them asked, "You from around here?" To which Mike quickly replied, "No, we're just passing through." Apparently satisfied, they nodded, pulled out, and rode away. A strange, tense, brief encounter. Our minds were made up. We would ride on. Just like the day we crossed Arkansas and rode on in the night to Elk City, OK exactly one week before, after a long day in the saddle, we made the Meridian KOA at almost the same time exactly as last Sunday- 9:45pm. We also had a cabin just like last week too. Many parallels.

Weather is looking rough back home for Monday, so we may have to linger in Alabama some tomorrow. We'll see in the morning...

Monday, September 27

After checking out storm reports all over north Alabama and Georgia, we opted for Lisa's suggestion and rode south for Mobile and the Florida panhandle. Kathy, my wife's sister, had arranged for us to spend a night at their beachside condo in Perdido Key, so we took US 45, a beautiful, winding highway down to Mobile. We swung east onto I-10, crossed the Mobile Bay, then caught Hwy 59 down to Gulf Shores. We did something I've wanted to do for many years- we rolled a beachfront road, the sands, dunes, and beaches of the Gulf of Mexico off our right shoulder. The last time I had the opportunity to ride along beaches was in 1998, at Myrtle Beach Bike Week, and got rained on the whole way. Not memorable. But this time, it was. We took that road across the state line into Florida, and got platefuls of fried seafood at the Crab Trap Restaurant. We rolled into Beach Colony, the condo complex, and after tossing our gear in a couple of rooms, we took a sunset walk down the beach. What an amazing turnaround- who would have thought we'd wind up at the beach on this trip?? Mike observed, "We may have lost Arizona, but we gained Florida."

We met a lady clutching a puppy sitting on a towel by the shore, whose name was Julie. We struck up a conversation with her, and she shared with us that she lived alone in a mobile home nearby, with her puppy, finding odd jobs to pay the bills. Julie confided she was a 13-year recovering alcoholic, a born-again Christian, but estranged from her husband and children for many years, and unable to find permanent work. Yet in spite of all this, she had a positive view of life, and a deep trust in God, which gave her contentment. We had a moment of prayer with her there on the beach, the sun fading to our west, for her work, provision, and reunion with her children someday. She cried as we prayed over her. She declared, "I knew God was leading me to come down to the beach tonight, and now I know why: To meet and pray with a couple of biker brothers in the Lord. Thank you so much!" Again, I'm amazed at the people and stories we've discovered on this trip. God is good, all the time. And He is sovereign. We would have never been afforded this opportunity had we continued west, took another route home, or even timed our walk differently. Moments like these, and so many on this trip, were orchestrated by the hand of God.

The sunset over the Gulf to our west was brilliant, awash in color through small, scattered clouds on the horizon, and the subsequent moon and stars over the water was breathtaking. We were meant to be here, in this place, at this time. We'll leave for home in the morning, the final day and leg of our journey, but coming to the white, Gulf Coast beaches of north Florida was an unexpected pleasure, for sure.

Tuesday, September 28

Mike and I packed up, cleaned and tidied the place up for my sis-in-law, and said so long to the sunny, sandy shores of Perdido Key. We snaked our way through the outskirts of Pensacola, then pointed the bikes north to I-65. We rode hard to Montgomery, Alabama, then jumped on I-85 northeast back into "Georgia On My Mind"! We pulled over into Alabama's last rest stop before the state line, for a "rest" and refreshment break. Upon returning to the bikes, we met up with Terry, a state employee cleaning up the parking lot, admiring our motorcycles. We struck up a nice conversation with Terry, who showed us pictures on his phone of his '67 Camaro drag strip racer. "She's a screamer," he beamed. "I wouldn't want to run against her," Mike quipped, which brought a smile to Terry's lined face. He wished us a safe ride home, and with that, we crossed back into our home state of Georgia. We gunned the throttles to Atlanta, bypassed the downtown traffic on I-285, and dodged the crazy cagers on Hwy 78 past the "Big Rock" Stone Mountain, finally arriving home around 7:30pm. So good to be back home.

What an amazing odyssey this has been! Ten days, ten states, over 3300 miles roundtrip. We experienced the mountains of north Georgia, Tennessee and Arkansas, the rolling prairies of Oklahoma, the "fruited plains" of the Texas Panhandle, rode hundreds of miles on and alongside old Route 66, out into the mesas of New Mexico, back across Texas, across Louisiana and Mississippi, then the bright beaches of Alabama and Florida. We witnessed sights and wonders we could not have anticipated or planned for, met people we will always remember, and discovered the presence and hand of God everywhere we rode. Although we were never "standing on the corner in Winslow, Arizona" like we had hoped, we did indeed discover what it means to "get your kicks on Route 66"! New Mexico to the Gulf of Mexico, and so much in between. It was a great adventure, shared with a great friend, following our great Lord. To Him be all the thanks, credit and glory.

My Friends, Mike and David

After my big road trip last year with my friend Mike, I had looked forward to a new great adventure this year, whatever it might be. When plans to ride to Sturgis, SD with another friend fell through back in August, I was at a loss about what to do this year, or if I should even try a road trip at all. I still had plenty of time off, so Mike & I planned a short weekend trip together up to Asheville, North Carolina, to visit Freedom Biker Church. He only had a couple of days, so I planned to ride back into North Georgia to tent camp an extra day or two by myself. Sounded like a plan. We took off Saturday morning and rode out to Athens, then up Hwy. 441 into North Carolina. 441 is a beautiful road that I never get tired of riding, leading up into the mountains and beyond. We arrived mid-afternoon at a KOA campground east of Asheville, unloaded, then rode over to the location of the biker church, to ensure we knew where it was. After supper at a 50's style diner, we spent a peaceful evening around a campfire at the KOA with some wonderful people- Kevin & Linda from Hickory, NC, dedicated Christians and youth leaders in their church; and Jeremy & Serena from Greenville, SC, with their two cute little boys. Wonderful conversation for hours, and my first campfire of the fall!
Before turning in for the night, I posted a couple of pictures on

Facebook of our trip so far, and within minutes got a message from an old high school friend, David Lunsford, inviting me over to Sevierville, TN for a couple of days. We had reconnected on FB about two years ago, but had not seen or even spoken to each other in the 30+ years since we graduated high school. I called the number he sent me, and he said, "Forget camping, I've got a nice, cozy bed up here in Pokeberry Hollow for ya!" This trip just took a turn into a whole new adventure, I thought to myself.

David and I had been classmates off and on throughout our elementary years, and had been skateboard bros throughout our junior high and early high school years. Our lives diverged in 10th grade, as he sank into drugs and alcohol abuse, and I gave my life to Christ. As I went on to college, seminary, and into marriage and ministry, David's life sank deeper over the years. After multiple rehab and detox stints, and two failed marriages, he found himself face down in his cabin aboard a freighter ship he worked on down in Florida, and he surrendered his life to Jesus Christ in 1998. He stood up a new man, he told me, a "new creation" as 2 Corinthians 5:17 proclaims.

So here I was, spending a couple of days with my long-lost (literally) adolescent friend, now brother in Christ as well! He and his wife Donna welcomed me into their home like family- which spiritually we had become. We spent the next 2 1/2 days eating out, seeing sights around Gatlinburg and Pigeon Forge, and helping him with chores around Pokeberry Hollow, their breathtakingly beautiful homestead in the hills. We even spent an afternoon playing in his creek like two school kids, building dams and catching crawfish. Every morning and evening was spent on their front porch, reminiscing and laughing, talking about Christ, while the sweet smell of his wild cherry pipe smoke floated through the air.

Finally on Tuesday morning, I packed up, we prayed together, and

I rode south toward home. Running south on 441 out of Gatlinburg, I rode through the Great Smoky Mountains National Park. The morning mist was still rising off the mountains, and the sun cast brilliant beams down through the trees as I rode, like a scene in Rivendell from Lord of the Rings. It was captivating, almost holy. I would break out to scenic overlooks periodically, and could see out across the Smokies as the clouds still hung low in the valleys. Nothing quite like riding above the clouds. I rode and worshipped God all the way across the 40+ miles through the park.

Crossing back through a sliver of NC before returning into Georgia, the sun was brilliant and the temps were getting warmer. I finally arrived home around 3:30pm, to an empty house, with Lisa still at work and Kelsey at school. I spent some time unpacking, unwinding, and reflecting on the trip. No regrets, no disappointments. When God closed one door (Sturgis), He opened another (Asheville, Sevierville). And I still got to spend time with two close friends- Mike, one of my current best friends, and David, an old friend and new brother in Christ. God has blessed more than I could have imagined. I am filled, and my cup runneth over.

Half-Century Road Trip

Last weekend I completed an epic road trip with my childhood friend Lyle Branton. We both are now 50 years old, and planned to motorcycle ride across the southern states, with specific objectives being riding the scenic Natchez Trace Parkway end to end, and riding across the entire panhandle of Florida beach front. We met up north of Atlanta on Sunday, September 22, and rode through the foothills of north Georgia, through the beautiful valley of Chattanooga, then across the remaining Appalachians to

Nashville. Tent camping for the night by a pristine lake, we rode west Monday to the north terminus of the Parkway, first enjoying the food and country music nostalgia of the famed Loveless Café. Then we started down our first stretch of the Parkway.

The Natchez Trace Parkway is approximately 444 miles long, winding through the hill country of Tennessee, down through the northwest corner of Alabama, then all the way across Mississippi to Natchez. We rode as far as Tishomingo, and made camp in a state park, again on a beautiful lake with the moon rising over the waters. We awoke to grey skies and drizzle on Tuesday, and got as far as Tupelo before hard rain forced us to hold up in a gas station/barbeque joint for two hours. When the worst had passed over the Parkway, we continued on, still in rain, but by the time we arrived in Jackson, the storm had cleared. We dried out in a hotel that night, and hit the road Wednesday morning in clear skies and warm temps to complete our journey down the Parkway. Finally reaching the famed road's southern terminus, we celebrated in Natchez with tamales at the local fave, Fat Mama's. After a some photos down by the Mississippi River, we blasted east across the state on Hwy 98, making for Mobile, AL, for an evening with my friend Greg Sweatt's dad.

Our journey along coastline began as we crossed Mobile Bay bridge at sunset. The colors in the sky were unlike any I had ever seen- all the pastels of the color palette were present, from bright gold of the setting sun, to brilliant orange, red, purple, various blues, even green, all reflected in the glass-like surface of the bay. Breathtaking. We spent a wonderful evening and

Thursday morning with Mr. Sweatt, then loaded up and ran south through Fair Hope, then Foley, Gulf Shores, Orange Beach, and on into Florida. We passed through Perdido Key, where my sister-in-law had a condo for several years, then Pensacola, Fort Walton, Destin, and made camp just off the beach at Topsail Hills State

Park.

Friday we rode through Seaside, Laguna Beach, then Panama City. Finally beyond the tourism part of the Panhandle, we rode beachfront through quaint little coastal and fishing towns, around the "Big Bend" of what locals call "Old Florida". This was to be my favorite leg of our whole ride. Mexico Beach, Port St. Joe, Apalachicola, Eastpoint and Carabella, all with vistas out across panhandle islands, peninsulas and keys. We crossed towering bridges over wide expanses of water, beheld tidal flats and rocky shorelines, under deep blue skies. I rode much of Big Bend in silent worship, unable to speak or even listen to music. The beauty was indescribable. We passed through Lanark Village and Panacea before swinging over to Perry, to spend a delightful evening with Lyle's oldest sister Peggy and her husband Dick. Saturday we arose, said goodbyes to our wonderful hosts, and rode one last time down to the Gulf of Mexico, about a mile behind Peggy and Dick's place. Swinging north, we throttled up out of Florida into south Georgia, and turned east along Hwy 84 through Quitman, Valdosta, Waycross, Jesup, and Hinesville, catching I-98 then I-16 into Savannah to my daughter Ansley's place for the night. We enjoyed watching UGA defeat LSU, ate at the popular Crab Shack out on Tybee Island, then got a good night's sleep before our final leg home.

Sunday we said goodbye to Ansley, Savannah, and the Atlantic Ocean and blasted west on I-16 for home. We parted ways in Dublin, he toward I-75 and Fayetteville, me up Hwy 441 to my folks in Eatonton and then on home to Dacula. This was a fantastic adventure with a nearly life-long friend, celebrating our half century out on the open road. Nearly 2100 total miles through five states, from the hills of Appalachia to the Mississippi River, across the Gulf coast and over to the Atlantic coast. "Epic" is the word I use to describe the trip. God guided us through beautiful places, to wonderful family and friends, and a four-decade friendship was deepened. Worth every minute and mile.

3 PEOPLE & PLACES

Plastic Jesus

I've been reading a book called, "Plastic Jesus" by Eric Sandras, which is about how we have reduced Christianity to a comfortable, packaged, "suburbia" faith, instead of the radical, life-changing, intimate purpose and relationship with Christ it was meant to be.

One section called, "Wearing Someone Else's Shirt", got me thinking last night. The author talked about how we often wear what we think or want to define us, but all too often we are living a lie. I thought of an example from this past week. Ansley had a knee surgery Thursday, and while I was at the surgical center, one of the nurses noticed my t-shirt, a Harley-Davidson shirt from Virginia a friend once gave me. She asked me, "Love your t-shirt!

Do you ride?" To which I replied, "Yes, I do." She then said, "My husband and I ride a Road King. What do you ride?" Suddenly, I was faced with a choice- Do I lie and say, "I ride a Heritage Classic" or something like that, or do I tell her the truth? She'll never know, I'll likely never see her again, and it's just a small conversation. I chose to be who I was, and told her, "I ride a Yamaha Royal Star- a poor man's Harley!" She exclaimed, "What a cool bike! I have a friend who rides one of those!" I chose honesty, and I'm glad I did.

Sandras says in his book, "Christians who are living in spiritual suburbia are 'just wearing the shirt.' We often profess to be followers of Christ, but are we really following Him into what He has called us to do? Are we fulfilling our unique, God-given purpose? Its possible to say all the right words, yet never surrender our hearts and wills to God's leading. God wants us to live out our calling; He doesn't just want us to wear His shirt." (p. 52). I want to live the life, not just wear the shirt.

Road Trip with Kelsey

This past Monday- Wednesday Kelsey & I did a short "Dad & Daughter" road trip up to Chattanooga, TN. We had a great time together- climbed all through Rock City, descended to Ruby Falls, visited the Tenn. Aquarium, toured Covenant College, strolled down the new Tennessee Riverwalk, and just had a great 3 days together. We needed the time together- it seems the older my girls get the busier we all are, and we often just see each other in passing. It was time well-spent.

As we left on Wednesday, I had made arrangements to visit Precept Ministries, right outside Chattanooga. This is the ministry headquarters of Kay Arthur, renowned Bible teacher and writer.

She has had a vast, influential ministry for decades, dating back to the late 60's. In fact, in 1974 she led my mother to Christ at a women's conference, who then pointed my dad to Christ in 1975, and I trusted Christ with Kay's help in 1979, as a 15 year old. Later, after high school, I spent a year living there, working in the ministry and sitting under Kay's teaching before returning home and beginning college. Kay is truly my "mother in the Lord", as well as for my own mom!

I didn't think Kay would remember me after all the years, but when she met us in the lobby, she lit up, bear-hugged me, and exclaimed, "Rob Brooks! It is so good to see you again! How many years has it been?!" We talked for about 45 minutes, just catching her up on my life, all God has done over the years and miles. Kay was very enthused to meet Kelsey, who really took to Kay immediately. She kept calling for staff members to come meet me, and some who knew me back then, still serving in the ministry there! It was an amazing time- a reunion of sorts. She wanted some pictures with us, saying she was so blessed to see me and know I was still walking with Christ, and passing on the faith to my girls and those in my ministry. Kay said, "Seeing you reminds me of the verse, 'I have no greater joy than knowing my children are walking in the truth.' You are like one of my boys!"

I was blessed immeasurably by this lady- to see and talk with her again, introduce my daughter to her, but mostly for the faith she brought to my family so many years ago. I know the Lord and am in the ministry, in no small part due to Kay Arthur's faithfulness to share Christ over the years. And I hope one day to enjoy seeing those I have influenced come back into my life, and see them still walking in the faith as well.

Choices, Consequences

Last night I had the opportunity to preach in a service the Spirit Riders & CMA put on with Chaplain Terry Buice, in the Gwinnett Prison. It was one of the larger services we've hosted there in some time- we had about 80 inmates attend it, and 8 men trusted in Jesus Christ. In the music, the prayer times, my sermon, and these men coming for salvation, we really felt God's presence in that prison. God is mending lives, even as they serve out their sentences.

An inmate approached me prior to the service, and gave me a necklace with a cross he had made, and wanted me to wear it as I preached, which I did. When everything was over, and all the inmates were being escorted back to their cells, he came back over to me and said, "Do you remember me? I used to go to First Baptist back when you were there." Suddenly I did remember him, and the times we had conversations over the years there. After I left and moved to Hebron, he just slipped from my memory, and here he was again, after all these years, standing before me in prison. My choices had led me further into God's kingdom work, and his choices had landed him behind bars. We talked for a moment, and he asked for prayer, that God would help him walk as a man of God again when he got out. I told him I certainly would.

As illusionist Brock Gill said when he was here, "Some choices you make don't matter. Some you make are life and death..."

Riding with Old Friends

The past 3 days I spent part of my vacation in the North Georgia mountains, motorcycle riding with 2 old high school friends, Lyle & Jimmy. We get our families together every summer and every

Christmas holiday, and have long talked about doing a road trip together. We met up at Jimmy's house in Alpharetta Sunday at 2pm, then took country roads up the state to Hiawassee, up near the state line. Jimmy's dad has a mountaintop cottage there, and I definitely fell in love with Hiawassee. It is a beautiful mountain town, on the shores of Lake Chatuge, a beautiful mountain lake. I want to live there someday!

We got up Monday morning and took off, following tranquil, scenic country roads over mountains and through valleys. The weather was sunny, breezy, & cool- perfect riding conditions. I always love riding up in the mountains- it seems to untangle my mind & heart. I worship Christ while I ride- so much beauty to behold. We rode & rode & rode...

Then Lyle's bike broke down. Late in the day, on our way back to town for a supper break, the bike just died at a stop sign. Nothing we could do kept it running. We roll-started it down a couple of hills, pushed it across a parking lot in town, and finally got it up to the cottage, coughing and hacking all the way. We never got it started again. Bummer...

Tuesday we got up late, cooked breakfast, cleaned the place up, then packed for home. Sadly, we were going back one bike short- we had to leave Lyle's bike behind at the cottage. Lyle rode with Jimmy for the first half of the trip home, and with me the last half. Kinda awkward, but we had to get him home!

We stopped up at an overlook on Hwy 9, where the Appalachian Trail crossed the road, outside of Dahlonega. We walked some of the Trail, just to say we did, and found a wild apple tree near the parking lot. The apples were small, red, and delicious. We kept to the country roads all the way back to Jimmy's house, arriving by 7pm.

Although the ride was cut somewhat short by a broken bike, it was still worth the time spent with old friends.

The older we get, the busier our lives get, the more intentional we have to be about keeping our friendships strong. I'm glad Lyle, Jimmy & I have stayed close friends over the years. Any time we can get together is time well spent.

Compassion

As I try to focus my heart more on Christ this new year, and "walk humbly before your God" like Micah 6:8 says, I've asked God to give me His eyes for other people, and grow my compassion for them. I get so hurried in my life, and so focused on my schedule, my agenda, etc., that I can easily pass people by, brush them off, without stopping to invest the love of God in them. I want to change that.

Well, God put me to the test right away, and gave me opportunities to be compassionate. And I failed miserably a couple of times. First, a young man who used to be in our children's ministry came by to visit me in the RockiTown room early Sunday morning, while I was working to get everything set up for the morning worship hours. I was less than glad to see him, and was not as friendly to him as I could have been. After some small talk, while I was still working away, he quietly said goodbye, and slipped out of the room. Then at the end of the morning, as the last of the kids had left for the day, a dad came through, who serves in the Army reserves and got back from Iraq in the past year. He asked for prayer in reconnecting with his 8-year old son, and for wisdom in dealing with some rebellion & respect issues they were beginning to have with him. I was finishing the process of putting everything away, and was tired at the end of a long morning (7am to 12:30pm), and gave him the customary "I'll pray for you", with some words of "every parent deals with these, welcome to parenthood" platitudes.

I was later so convicted over both encounters. I missed two opportunities to show compassion. It bummed me out for a couple of days.

Then today at the gym, I saw this lady that I had seen there before, and recognized from somewhere. She had looked at me before like she recognized me as well. As I saw her again today, I realized she worked at the gym, but instead of hurrying back to the office, and rather than passing by her and just saying, "Hi, how are you, good to see you" like we so often do, I stopped and asked her if we knew each other. Turns out, her family had attended my former church back in the 90's, and her two older kids had come up through my children's ministry there. Wow, that was how we knew each other! I asked her how the family was doing, and she proceeded to confide in me that her marriage fell apart about 8 years ago, she had struggled to provide for her 3 kids over the years, had lost a job in nursing that she had trained for, and only recently began work at the gym. I asked if she was attending that church still, and she said she had not been back since the divorce. She told me that she used to teach in preschool there, was involved in Adult Sunday School ministry, went to visitation every week, and never missed a worship service. Yet when her marriage and family was in crisis, no one ever contacted them to find out what was happening, or to say that they were missed. She relocated her kids up to Dacula, but had not plugged back into any church since.

So here was this woman whom I had once ministered to her children, dealing with the pain of a divorce and the pain of neglect from a church she had once faithfully served, coupled with the ongoing struggles of being a single mom. God kept me there listening to her, in the lobby of the gym, while she confided these things to her kids' old children's pastor from years ago. She finally had to get back to work, and only then did I say I'd pray for her and her family, and that we'll talk again sometime.

I left there today praying for her, and asking God, "Give me your eyes for the broken-hearted, and the compassion to not pass them by." Jesus would be in a crowd of people, and notice someone to the side who needed His touch, or someone who needed His attention. He always stopped, always made time, no matter who or what was pressing Him to keep moving.

Father, I want to stop for people more, and give them the love and life they need, from Your heart, through mine, to theirs.

Fill me with compassion.

Bad Example

I was off yesterday, the weather was finally good, so I lit out for a day of riding up in the north Georgia mountains. The further north I went, the higher in elevation I rose, the more the temperature cooled, aided by cloud cover over the mountains. I was glad I brought some layers under my leathers.

I stopped at a gas station outside Clermont, to warm up with a cup of coffee. As I stood in line to pay up, a woman entered with 2 boys, who looked about 15 and 10. I don't know if she was their mother or not, but they went to the back of the store, and came to the front carrying big cases of beer! All three were carrying them- each toted a case up. As they stood in line, I looked at her, the case she carried, then each of the boys, and their cases. I was shocked that this woman was bringing these boys along, and using them for this purpose. Not only that, as they approached the register next to me, the woman said, "Hi, back again! We took the last of your cases." The cashier said, "Looks like a huge party." To which she replied, "Oh yeah, the beer's gonna flow!" The boys were giggling behind her, holding their beer cases.

I couldn't believe all I had just seen and heard. What an absolutely terrible example she was setting with these boys. They were being set up for a life of drinking & drunkenness at an early age, not only by what they apparently see all the time, but forced to get involved in. Pathetic.

I hope and pray my life never leads others astray- intentionally or by accident. The Bible says, "It would be better for him to be thrown into the sea with a millstone tied around his neck than for him to cause one of these little ones to sin." Luke 17:2

Lyle's Dad

Last week, the father of one of my life-long friends passed away somewhat suddenly. It shocked and saddened me to hear the news. Lyle has been my closest friend since we were both 11 years old, and growing up, we spent a lot of time at each other's homes. I always loved and respected his parents immensely, and my parents always loved Lyle like another son.

Lyle's dad was always very encouraging and supportive. Lyle and I both participated in several sports, and Mr. Branton never missed an event, it seemed. He was always in the bleachers, cheering on his son, and me as well. In fact, I remember many wrestling meets where he and my dad would sit together, yelling all through Lyle's match, then all through mine! They would both be hoarse the day after. Fun memories.

"Mr. B" was also a great man of God. The times I spent the night at their home, I sat in on their nightly family devotionals. He apparently held these daily or nightly, until all 3 kids had moved out on their own. That's convicting to me- I'm in the ministry, and I feel so inconsistent in pulling my own family together for Bible/prayer times!

Mr. B not only walked the walk, he talked the talk. Everywhere he was- whether at the family store, out on business, at a restaurant, or in the prisons he so often chaplained in- Mr. B found a way to share the love of Christ with people. It was not uncommon for him to help lead a person to Christ, right wherever they were! And being a Gideon, he always had a Bible to give. Even in his waning years, in and out of hospitals with various health issues, he shared the love of Christ with people, in word and deed.

That heritage has been passed on to his family. Lyle is a strong Christian, as are his sister and brother. In fact, all the grandkids are now believers as well. All due in no small part to the life and witness of Mr. Lamar Branton. He followed God, and brought others along.

May I always strive to leave a legacy like that- in my family, and anyone God brings across my path. In the end, it's all that will really matter.

Isle of Man TT

I recently purchased online a DVD of the 2007 Isle of Man TT motorcycle race- one of the oldest, fastest, and wildest motorcycle road races on the planet. 2007 was the 100 year anniversary of the famed race, which takes place on the Isle of Man, a small island off the west coast of England. The course winds 37.74 road miles around and across the island, through small towns, over wide open spaces, along the coasts, and up over the mountains. The TT takes place each May, across a week, with multiple motorcycle races and many festivities. Its quite a spectacle! I'd love to visit one year.

The riders race their bikes for multiple laps around the small island, racing against the clock as much as each other. There are long straight-aways, and its amazing the speeds they reach on their 2-wheeled rockets! One particular rider, John McGuinness, is considered a legend of the TT. By the time the 2007 TT was over, he had achieved two milestones- he became one of the most decorated riders in TT history with 13 career wins, and he broke the all-time lap average speed, topping 130mph lap average in the final race. And best of all, **he is not much younger than me**! Hey, who says you have to slow down with age??

As I watched these races, I was mesmerized by the speed, control, focus, and determination of these human rockets. The greatest riders showed a precision and fire that carried them to great achievements, and to the few best, the winner's stand. I noted as well those who faded and failed. There were men who lost focus and fell behind, those who messed up and crashed, some who failed to calculate fuel usage properly and literally "gassed out", and others who had too-slow pit stops or mechanical breakdown, failing to place or even finish.

I was reminded of how similar a long race like the TT is like life in Christ. Many start "out of the gate" strong and fast, but slow down, get distracted, make wrong turns and poor choices, and "crash" their lives, or just pull over and quit. It seems like so many I've known over the years have wound up this way. As I travel life's road, I see the wreckage of lives that had so much promise, but self-destructed. I see lives just coasting along, not aiming at anything, much less winning. And I see those who have quit, and walked away. They all break my heart, but make me more determined to ride hard, stay focused on Christ, and finish strong. The writer of Hebrews said it well in chapter 12:1 & 2- "...let us run with perseverance the race that is marked out for us. Let us fix our eyes on Jesus..."

I don't want to end up a "wreck". I don't want to just coast along, aimless. And I certainly don't want to quit and walk away. I want to live my life by those verses, and so many others in the Bible, that challenge me to follow Christ, hard and fast, all the way to the finish line. And there, I want to see Him face-to-face, and hear him say, "Well done, My son! I'm proud of you", as I stand with all the hosts of Heaven, celebrating in the "winner's circle." (2 Timothy 4:8). That keeps me going.

Hellos and Goodbyes

Yesterday I spent some time both at a NICU ward in a hospital, and a funeral home. A day of hellos and goodbyes. I first visited the neo-natal unit at Eastside Hospital to celebrate the birth of a friend's new son, born somewhat premature but doing well. The parents had stepped out, so I missed them, but was allowed to scrub up, robe up, and visit little Caden, barely 2 pounds. He was so tiny! His head fit in the palm of my hand, and his fingers were too small to wrap around one of my fingers. Yet he was getting larger and stronger by the day, hopefully going home in a couple of weeks, once he puts a little more size on. I gently covered him with my hands and prayed over him, for his health and growth, for his family, and for his salvation one day. It was a wonderful few moments with this tiny, new life.

By the end of the day, I rode over to a funeral home to pay my respects to another family friend, who lost her father over the weekend. Vicki and her husband Daryl told me her father, who had recently hit 79, had been a life-long follower of Christ, and had always been a godly example to his kids, his grand kids, his church, and everyone he had influence with over the years. What a rich legacy to leave behind! The place was packed- and had been all day, I understand. Daryl told me that he had woke up about 3am Sunday morning, checked his blood pressure, read a little in his rocker, then apparently slumped over and went home to Heaven. "Precious in the sight of the Lord is the death of His saints." Psalm 116:15

So, one man's sunset is another man's dawn. I reflected on the day later that evening, swinging on the front porch as the sun fell beyond the tree line. Here I am in the middle- miles & years away from birth and youth, and hopefully miles and years away from my end here as well. And I was reminded of another Bible passage, for the road ahead- "Teach us to number our days, that we may gain a heart of wisdom." Psalm 90:12

God bless the road, from cradle to grave.

A Second Bike

This past weekend, I bought a second motorcycle. Its a 2001 Kawasaki ZR-7s, a small, lightweight 750cc bike. I first became interested in this particular model about 2 years ago, after seeing one at a motorcycle shop in Watkinsville. I had never seen one before, and began to study them on the web. Kawasaki only made them for the US market from 2000 to 2004, but they were a very well-rounded motorcycle. Plenty of power, great handling, easy to maintain, and could run about 300 miles on a tank of gas. I've been thinking about a small, cheap second bike for some time, when we had the money, and recently Lisa told me, "we have some extra cash, why don't you go find one?" Oh yeah...

I began to search for them on the web, for the better part of three months. They are hard to find, having only been produced for such a short time. They also tend to run from $2500-3500, but one day last week, I saw this one come up. The bike was in east Tennessee, had 19k miles, and was being offered for $2000. I had to check it out. I emailed and texted back and forth with the owner, found out all about it, and asked a friend of mine, Tommy, to ride up with me to have a look.

We set out Saturday morning, Sept. 8, my birthday. It took over four hours to arrive in the owner's town. We were in rain most of the drive up and home, but the sun broke through as we pulled into his parking lot. Turns out, Jesse the owner was a Christian, and lived/worked for a church-run drug and alcohol rehab center that was operated by his family and their church. I rode the bike around, looked it all over, and we negotiated a price. We agreed on $1700, and I was thrilled. It needed some TLC, but was worth every penny of that. I saved $300 as well, which would make my wife happy!

The great part was meeting and dealing with a Christian brother, who was doing a good work in people's lives. The ministry is called "Place of Hope", and before we left, we all prayed together, for each other's ministries. It was a perfect way to end our meeting. We got home, unloaded the bike, and I thanked Tommy for accompanying and helping me. Our time together talking up and back was as much a blessing as buying the bike and meeting Jesse. Tommy is a dear bro in Christ, and I enjoyed every moment of the day with him. The whole experience was a God-blessed time.

I thanked God for the opportunity to own this fun little bike, and dedicated it to the Lord just like I did the Royal Star so many years ago. God has used that bike to allow me to go places, meet people, and participate in ministry beyond my wildest dreams. May this little ride be used by God to open up even more doors to enjoy and honor Him.

Life-long Friend

This past weekend, I got to ride and spend some time with my childhood friend Lyle Branton. We met Saturday down in Covington, about halfway between us. We ate a Cajun lunch at RL's Off The Square, me a plate of Jambalaya, Lyle a Grouper plate. His bill: about $35. Mine: $8. Ha! We sat and talked for about an hour, catching up on each other's families, work, and personal lives from the past year. Great conversation over a great meal.

We hopped on our moto-bikes and rode out country roads toward Rutledge, a quaint little town on the way to Madison with a great ice cream shop. By the time we approached the city limits, a lumbering, 3mph, mile-long train was rolling through, blocking our way into the town! Dang, no ice cream in Rutledge.

We blasted east on State Road 12 through rolling hills and dairy farms, woods and wide open farm land. All in bright sunshine, cool temps. We finally arrived in the historic town of Madison, the city "too pretty to burn" according to Union General Grant in the Civil War. We pulled up to the original Scoops ice cream parlor, got a couple of cones, and sat outside in the sunshine to catch up some more. We talked about middle age, the "second half", and what God might be leading us into for the years ahead.

We were within 30 miles of my parent's lake house, so we decided to ride south to Eatonton. We pulled up in their driveway about 2:30pm, and spent a couple of hours talking, laughing, and reminiscing with my folks on the back porch, over sweet tea and homemade cookies. We finally saddled up for home and rode back toward Eatonton, where Lyle headed west for Fayetteville, and I made my way north for Dacula. A day well-spent.

Lyle and I first met at 11 years old, as 7th graders. He had just moved to Fayetteville from Tifton, Ga with his family, and didn't know a soul yet. I was paired up with him as a locker partner, and we struck up an instant friendship. We ran track together, joined some of the same school clubs, and by high school were both on the wrestling squad and cross-country team. Through it all, we stayed locker partners as well, hung out at each other's house after school and on weekends, and participated in each other's church youth groups regularly.

Even though we went our separate ways for college, we stayed in touch, were involved in each other's weddings, and were there for the birth of each other's children. We even spent a few years at the same church in Clarkston Ga, me as the youth pastor, Lyle as a deacon. We have been there for nearly all of the major events in each other's lives and families. Even when there were years that we didn't get to spend as much time together, our families always met up for Christmas, New Years, or summer getaways at the lake, with Jimmy and Carla Jimmerson, another couple we have been close to since high school.

Lyle has seen much pain and anxiety over the past several years-the loss of the family business, job loss of his wife, both now embarking on new career paths, the death of his godly father, a son on tour of duty in Iraq, and painful struggles in his extended family. Yet through it all, like Job in the Bible, Lyle has maintained his integrity, kept his faith in God. As he has told me before, "God's got us, we're in good hands." Good hands indeed.

Lyle inspires me, always has. I may be the one in vocational ministry, but to me, he is the spiritual giant. I guess adversity can do that. Pain and suffering will either make your faith, or break it. Depends on what that faith is founded upon. Lyle's faith is founded, grounded in Christ. May I always anchor my soul to Him as well.

Thankfulness and Generosity

Yesterday I found myself interacting with several people in various states of need in their lives, with the opportunity to help and encourage each in some way.

Every year, our church collects food for needy families, packing them Thanksgiving boxes with turkey, dressing, and everything else for a full family meal. I swear, Hebron is the most generous church I've ever seen. Numerous families came by to pick up their boxes, each profusely grateful. We even had the privilege of quietly packing a couple of boxes for one of our very faithful children's ministry leaders, whose family has fallen on hard times in recent years. Humbling, to serve him and his family, in light of all they have done over the years for this ministry.

Later, I rode over to an older gentleman's house I had met the other night at a Redbox station, who had a couple of old motorcycles to sell. I examined his two bikes, but also noted he walked with a limp and a cane. When I inquired, he confided, "I'm 71 years old, and have had a couple of lower back surgeries in the past couple of years. Bone on bone down there. In fact, I'm facing a possible hip replacement this coming year, if we can afford it. I just can't get down and work on these bikes anymore, much less ride them. Time to let them go." I could sense the sadness in his voice- not only at having to give up riding, but also just at gradually losing his health, and ability to do the things he enjoys. I told him, "Well, whether we do business or not, God bless you, I'll be praying about all that for you, and I hope you have a great Thanksgiving with your family." He was very grateful.

Later that evening, I had to meet Lisa down in Snellville with the pickup truck, to pick up some furniture from a coworker of hers. At a gas station outside town, a woman pulled up alongside me in a beat-up old Toyota, and asked, "Sir, I hate to ask, but could you spare some change? I'm trying to get home to South Carolina for Thanksgiving, and am about out of money." I told her, "All I have is $3, I'm filling my truck up on a card, but I'll give you what I have. And I'll pray you get safely home. God bless you." She gave an emotional thank you, then pulled out and drove off.

I met Lisa at the apartment of her coworker, who was being evicted, unable to pay the rent anymore. We had given her a dining room set with six chairs, one we bought ourselves about 20 years ago. Now, she couldn't take it with her, moving into a much smaller place, but we said we'd store it for her, and when she could take it, we'd give it back to her. Again, she expressed heartfelt gratitude, for the gift to begin with, and the offer to give it back to her if/when she was ready.

We drove it to one of Lisa's friend's house, who said she had room in her basement to store it. She herself is a single mom with a daughter, no child support from her ex-husband (in prison), struggling to make ends meet and keep her home. She had hit something and broke the passenger side mirror on her car, and couldn't afford to fix it. I pulled off the broken one, and we told her we'd help get and install a new one for her.

Driving home, I was thinking about all these various people who had crossed paths with me today. I was grateful for all God has blessed my own family with, way more than we need or deserve. I also found myself grateful for the opportunity to serve, give, and encourage, to each of these very different people and life circumstances. I had been praying that God would stir up in me a heart of generosity, not only over the holidays, but as a way of life. I feel like I've become too selfish in recent years, gaining and keeping only for me and my family. I want to have a generous heart and an open hand with all God has blessed us with. "To whom much is given, much is required" Luke 12:48.

We are by no means wealthy by American standards, but certainly are compared to much of the rest of the world. If anyone should be a giving people, it should be Christians, those of us who have truly tasted of the goodness and generosity of the Lord.

What better way to show thankfulness?

An Amazing Turn of Events

It's been several weeks since the last post, and much has transpired.

Following up on the story last month of Mike, the older gentleman I met about the two motorcycles-

This story has progressed rapidly, in amazing ways. At first, Mike wanted $2K for Triumph (they go for $3K+ on the web), and $1K for Vulcan, but even then was willing to wiggle on prices, since neither had run in over a year. I told him I'd get back to him after Thanksgiving.

We talked on Monday of the next week, and he informed me he was taking his wife out of town to see her mother the first week of December. I asked if he would let me borrow the shop manual for the Triumph while he was gone, to see if I could figure out if there was anything else wrong with the bike, aside from needing a new battery. Mike said, "I'll do better than that. I'll let you take the bike to your house, so you can work on it yourself. If you get it running, I'll come off the price even more, to comp you for your time, effort, and money. If you can't get it running and want to call it all off, I'll comp you anyway." I jumped at the chance! Jack Butler, one of my riding buddies, brought his trailer, and we picked it up. Mike's wife, Donna, wanted him to follow us to my house, saying, "Sorry, but I'm not as trusting as Mike is!" Hoping to find an opening to maybe share my faith some with Mike, I said, "That is no problem at all! In fact, I hope you can trust preachers, because I'm one of them over at Hebron. So you'll be able to track me down at my home, or my church." As I handed them my card, they both lit up, and Mike declared, "What a blessing from God! I'm a Messianic Jew, gave my life to Christ over 20 years ago!" Wow! I was blown away. No doubt in my mind, ours had not been a chance meeting at that Red Box the week before.

We got the bike to my house, moved into my basement shop, and

Mike offered to give me a ride back to the church. I obliged, thanked Jack, and hopped in Mike's truck. We talked family, careers, and Christ all the way back to Hebron. Pulling into the parking lot, Mike saw my red ZR7s sitting there, and asked to see it. He walked all around it, admiring the little ride, and asked to sit on it. "Sure, throw a leg over," I told him. He lit up again as he straddled it, saying, "Wow, it's so light and well-balanced. And I can touch ground easy on it." He stepped off, stood there in thought for a moment, then asked, "Would you consider a trade? If you can get the Triumph running, I'd like to swap with you. On this bike, I think I might have a few more riding years in me." Surprised, I said, "Absolutely! I'd love that Triumph. I get her running, you got a deal." He said he'd bring a new battery by the church for me the next day, and we shook on it.

Sure enough, Thursday he met me with the battery. We stood and talked for about 30 minutes outside, then he declared, "I have a little revision to my proposal, if you are open to it. I'd still like to straight trade with you, and I'm willing to throw in the Vulcan 1500 too. So I'll give you both bikes for your ZR." I was stunned. Two bikes for one! Triumph for ZR, and basically the 1500 for free! Incredible. I nearly hugged the man. I told him, "Let me see what I can do with the Triumph while you are gone, and if all goes well, when you get back we'll see about closing the deal."

Well, to make a long story short, over the next two evenings, and half a Saturday with my dad's help, we got that Triumph running and tuned. In the meantime, I did some wrenching and cleaning on the ZR, so it would be ready for Mike. Upon his return, he met me at our house, and we went for a 30 minute ride- me on the Triumph, Mike on the ZR, so he could get a good feel for it. He had not ridden a motorcycle in a year and a half, so we said a prayer together, then took it easy out on some nice country roads I knew he'd enjoy. Upon returning, he stated, "I love it. I want it. Let's do this." We shook on it, agreeing to swap titles early the next week, and finalize everything.

So here I am on Sunday night, marveling at God's hand in all of this. I've had a dream as of late to turn my love for motorcycling into a profit, by writing articles for motorcycle and Christian magazines, and "flipping" bikes on the side- finding ones like these, sitting idle in garages, needing just a little TLC to get them on the road again, buy them low, resell them for profit, and make new friends along the way. Just like Mike. And here we are, getting a like-new Triumph Sprint in a swap, a basically free Kawasaki Vulcan 1500 to work on then sell, and I already have four articles set to run in about five different magazines across the winter, and more I'll be submitting soon. God is at work in this, and no telling where it will all go. But I'm excited, and ready to follow Him down this road.

4 SIGHTS & SOUNDS

Gravestones

It was beautiful weather again today, so I went out for a ride again (big surprise). While riding, I came upon an old graveyard behind a little country church. You might think this is strange, but I like walking through old cemeteries- you can read a lot of history in the gravestones. I parked and walked among the plots, and found many fascinating ones- A Civil War veteran who served under Gen. Robert E. Lee; a family that lost 4 children in a span of 8 years back at the turn of the century; a pastor who had served in the same church for almost 50 years; a soldier who died in WWI and was laid to rest here; a child died at age 6, marked with a stone angel; A woman who lived to be 104 years old. Amazing... And so many others, each representing a life lived here, a person loved there. What were their lives like? What memories did they leave behind for others? I was reminded how fleeting life is, how fragile it is. Whatever years I have here, I want them to be spent in love- for my Lord and Father, for my wife and girls, for my family and friends, for those in my sphere of ministry, for those who cross paths with me. Just to live and give the life and love of Jesus Christ. I hope my gravestone will one day read- "He Loved: His Lord, his family, his fellow man."

"Life is but a vapor, here one moment and gone the next..." James 4:14

Heaven's Beauty

I love the colors of fall. I'm amazed and dazzled every year by the incredible display of hues in creation. From bright yellows, to neon oranges, and rich reds, no artist ever painted with more vivid colors. As far as the beauty you can see in creation, I think I enjoy the fall more than the spring. There are even flowers blooming in the fall, adding to the brilliance! Over the past couple of weekends, I've ridden my motorcycle on short trips around North Georgia, and have been awed by the colors everywhere: God's ever-changing canvas on the mountains, hills, fields, and the sky. As the late songwriter Rich Mullins penned, "There's so much beauty around us, for just two eyes to see; but everywhere I go, I'm looking..."

I believe Heaven's beauty will truly be beyond our comprehension. I believe God's heavens and earth will be perfected and free from death, decay, and disruption. I can't say this for sure, but I believe the new earth will display all the colors of spring, summer and fall, altogether. Imagine for instance- a cherry blossom tree with its white flowers out, and its leaves fully orange, at the same time! In fact, all the flowering trees and plants, in full bloom and full fall color, set against the greens of evergreens, and the bluest skies ever seen- forever.

54

I'm just imagining, as I sit here and gaze out my front porch window...

"According to His promise we are looking for new heavens and a new earth, in which righteousness dwells." 2 Peter 3:13

The Bridge

Today I took a ride with several Spirit Riders friends out to Comer, Ga., to the Watson Mill Bridge. This is one of the oldest covered bridges in the state, and was featured in the movie, "The Bridges of Madison County." It was built in the late 1800's, and was restored about 30 years ago. I always enjoy historical places, and this bridge trip was very enjoyable. With the leaves falling off the trees, and the weather getting colder, it's time to get out and enjoy the sights and sounds while you can.

In His Presence

Last night as I left for church, the sky was gently raining, a cool breeze was blowing, and I saw 5 deer down my driveway, by the woods. They just stood there looking at me as I slowly rode past. Just beyond, a large rabbit popped out by the driveway, stopped to eyeball me for a moment, then scampered across into the fields on the other side. I rode on to church in silence, feeling as though I was already in the presence of God.

At church, we had a quiet, prayer and praise-filled service, with peaceful songs of worship and corporate prayer times, both at the altar and at our seats. I felt the presence of God strongly there too, among His people gathered before Him.

I don't know which is more beautiful, more moving- the harmony of His creation, or the assembling of His saints.

God wants us to not just relegate our encounters with Him to once or twice a week, but to see Him in our everyday experiences, and commune with Him among His people, and in His creation. Living & walking in His presence,

Wrong Message

The other day, Ansley & I went for a motorcycle ride. We passed by an old, small church building, with a message sign out by the roadside. This is what the sign said-
"The weather never changes in hell"
- Friendship Baptist Church
I found the words on that sign ironic. A church with such a friendly name, yet such a cold-hearted message. I find it sad that this message is what everyone driving by this church will judge those people by- and some will judge the rest of Christianity by that message as well. So much for "Friendship"...
Its not that the message is untrue- The Bible has much to say about hell, as much as it does about Heaven. But that's not the point. If that's all people see or hear of the message of Christ, it certainly is grossly inadequate. So often, the media portrays Christians as ignorant, narrow-minded, and mean-spirited. When messages like that sign are what people see, it feeds that false stereotype. I'm sure the people in that church are sweet, kind, and generous. Sadly, most people will never know that about those people- or the rest of us.
People in churches that display messages like that must think they are being real clever... me, as a Christ-follower who wants people to see and hear the life and love of Jesus in me, I find that sign message offensive. I certainly don't envision anyone seeing that sign, turning in, bursting in the door, and begging someone to tell them about Jesus Christ. BTW- I've never even seen anyone there, even if someone did stop in for help.
We have the greatest message in the history of the universe-

salvation, forgiveness, and restoration found in Jesus Christ. We must be so careful to present the whole Gospel, especially in our own lives. I want my life- my words, my actions, my attitudes, etc- to attract people to Jesus Christ, not give them more reasons to scorn.

"Let your light so shine before men, that they may see your good deeds, and glorify your Father in Heaven."- Jesus

Restoration

I'm home sick today, its Monday, an unusually warm February day, and I'm fighting a head/chest infection. No fun.
My old friend David Lunsford sent me this remedy-
"A big bowl of chicken soup, followed by a 60-mile motorcycle ride in the country always makes me feel better. If that doesn't work follow up with 40 pages Brennan Manning, taken along with 6 tracks of Rich Mullins. A guaranteed cure for whatever's got you down." Sounds like a cure to me!!
I was thumbing through some devotional readings I've compiled from John Eldredge and others, and came across one called, "Restoration". It struck a chord in my heart today, I guess due to the combination of my illness, the warm day, and my longings for spring to get here. Here's a few thoughts from it-
"The blind saw, the deaf heard, the lame walked, the dead were raised. Wherever humanity was broken, Jesus restored it. He is giving us an illustration here, and there, and there again. The coming of the kingdom of God restores the world he made."
"God has been whispering this secret to us through creation itself, every year, at springtime, ever since we left the Garden... After months and months of winter, I long for the return of summer. Sunshine, warmth, color, and the long days of adventure together. The garden blossoms in all its beauty. The meadows soft

and green. Vacation. Holiday. Isn't this what we most deeply long for? To leave the winter of the world behind, what Shakespeare called 'the winter of our discontent,' and find ourselves suddenly in the open meadows of summer?"

"The restoration of the world played out before us each spring and summer is precisely what God is promising us about our lives. Every miracle Jesus ever did was pointing to this Restoration, the day he makes all things new."

(exerpts from "Epic", by John Eldredge)

Restoration- that is what Jesus' mission was all about, what His crucifixion accomplished, what it means to walk with Christ in this life, and ultimately, what we set our heart and hope on for our eternity. The ultimate restoration of all things. "Behold, I make all things new", says Jesus in Revelation 21:5.

Scars to Stars

Today marked the 9-year anniversary of my motorcycle accident. I'd almost forgot, until Ansley reminded me yesterday that it would be. Interestingly, she was delivering a speech in one of her college classes on motorcycle safety today, which I had helped her research over the weekend, when she suddenly realized, "Hey Dad, I'll be making this speech exactly 9 years to the day after your accident!" It seemed so many years ago now, as I recounted the events of that day for her speech.

I had taken today off, due to a busy weekend of visiting hospitals & funeral homes as the weekend on-call pastor. After finishing some morning yard work, I hopped on the bike and took off for an afternoon of riding. I can think of no better way to commemorate that fateful day 9 years ago, than a good ride on a beautiful day. I headed southeast toward Bethlehem, then through Statham, then down to Watkinsville. I stopped in at NPR Ducati, gawking at the cool Italian bikes on display. One day, I hope to own a 2nd bike, maybe a Ducati Monster 620 or 695. Lord willing, of course... It was a peaceful, relaxing ride through the country, down roads largely deserted. I rode and prayed, as I often do, about anything and anyone God brought to mind. I also spent time reflecting on the accident nine years ago. An inattentive motorist had jumped out into traffic, trying to get across to the opposite lanes, and instead jumped into my path. I'd had precious little time to react, gripping down on both brakes in an effort to reduce as much speed as possible, all in a split second. I'd hit him at his left front headlight, flipped over his hood, and landed about 10 feet beyond, in oncoming traffic. Thankfully, cars stopped fast, and many came to my aid. I suffered a compound fracture of my left femur, a shattered kneecap, bruised wrist and shoulder, and numerous cuts and scrapes. I endured 4 surgeries over 18 months, and months of physical therapy to learn how to walk again.

I had always feared two things from the accident- first, that I would never be able to run and exercise again to the extent I was used to, and second, that I might never ride again. But God is faithful, and He allowed me to recover fully, and I've since been more active than before, and of course, I'm riding again, logging about 10K miles a year on the big Yamaha.

As I rode today, I reflected on these things, and how good God is. That accident not only made me a much safer rider, it also has opened so many doors to identify with and minister to people who suffer physically, esp. folks involved in accidents. God has truly turned my scars into stars, as an old preacher used to say. And I have my share of scars!

I love to ride motorcycles. I love the openness of it, being right out in the elements; I love the feel of a powerful machine under me, under my total control, blasting down the road; I love the wind in my face, the sun on the back of my neck, the sights, the smells, the sounds, the feeling of temperature changes up and down hills, the freedom. But most of all, I love the solitude, and the communion with my Father out on the road. I am thankful He gave me back my health, and thankful for this motorcycle He gave me, to enjoy riding, to enjoy Him, and to share His love with others I meet out there.

"We know that God causes all things to work together for the good of those who love Him, who have been called according to His purpose." Romans 8:28

Under the Stars

I'm on vacation this week, between the super-fun 5th Grade Adventure Trip we completed last week, and VBC coming up the end of July. No real plans for this week, just relaxing with my family, moto-riding down to my parent's place at Oconee, and getting a few much needed things done around the house.

The other night, I took a late-night walk down my long driveway, and lay down near the end of it. I spent some quiet time on my back, just staring up into space. Teddy sat down next to me, sniffing the air. A cool breeze blew up, and wafted over us. Suddenly, within moments of each other, two shooting stars streaked across the sky. It was amazing. Then a firefly hovered over me, and lit up several times before drifting away. It was all perfectly quiet, and perfectly peaceful. The breeze, the shooting stars, the firefly, my little furry friend by my side- a true "God moment" to linger in. This passage out of the Bible came to mind, out there under the stars-

"When I consider the heavens,

the work of Your hands,

the moon and stars

which You have set in place-

What is man that You are mindful of him?

the son of man that You care for him?

Yet You made him a little lower than the heavenly beings,

and crowned him with glory and honor." *Psalm 8:3-5*

Every time I hear some evolution-pushing "mad scientist", every time I see commercials on TV for shows peddling evolution propaganda ("The Missing Link-This Changes Everything", "Life After People", etc.), every time some so-called "scholar" screams into a camera, "we are all just cosmic accidents! We came from nothing, and we will go to NOTHING!" (BTW- that came from a scientist on the DVD "Exposed", about anti-creation bias in science)- I am reminded of these verses. There is a God who created all, who dearly loves us, who came for us in the form of Jesus Christ, and yes, has a purpose for our lives, here and beyond. Evolutionists can keep their cold, hopeless, depressing view of mankind, the world, and the universe. I know the God in control, and He will get the last laugh. In the meantime, I'll keep reading His words of life in the Bible, and I'll keep visiting with Him on star-filled, cool-breeze, meteor-streaked, firefly-lit, beautiful nights. It's an honor to know Him and enjoy Him.

Thorns and Thistles

Sometimes, cutting grass around my house really gets on my nerves. We have about 2 acres of land, and mowing my yard is often spread across a couple of days. I don't try to mow it every weekend, only about every 2 weeks. As the summer wears on, it seems I'm cutting more weeds than grass! Grass is hard to grow, and weeds are hard to kill. Example- my yard has so many patches of crabgrass, that I can cut it one week, and a week-10 days later, while the rest of the surrounding grass is still short, long spindly stems are growing up through the crabgrass, already 2+ ft. long. I've got thorny vines popping up everywhere, and I gave up a long time ago on trying to pull them up or kill them- I just mow over them as well, along with every other weird weed that pops up. Feels like an "exercise in futility", battling back the elements, holding off the "creeping green" every year. A never-ending chore, another reason to take a ride.

When I complain about it every week, I also remind myself, "A result of the fall." Biblically, it's true, actually- "creation was subjected to futility" (Romans 8:20) as a result of Adam's & Eve's sin, and expulsion from the Garden. Adam was condemned to toil in the dirt all the days of his life, struggling against "thorns and thistles", by the sweat of his brow (Genesis 3:17-19). Boy, I can identify some days...

I look forward to the day creation is redeemed and restored- "the creation itself will also be set free from its slavery to corruption into the freedom of the glory of the children of God" (Romans 8:21). That means perfection again, beauty fully restored, creation once again our ally, not our adversary. And no more cutting "my weeds."

Longing for Home

The other day, while driving back from Home Depot, I was struck by an amazing sunset. The sun was descending behind a large cloud, and casting color and light all over the sky. As I drove, it was in front of me, all the way home. I was listening to Switchfoot's song, "This is Home", and I prayed, "Father, thank You for the daily glimpses of Heaven You give me. This is one of the most beautiful sunsets I've ever seen. I long and ache for my true home that I've never seen. Thank You for the little hints from time to time. They take my breath away."

Then He unmistakably spoke to me, "Trust Me, you won't be disappointed. It will be beyond all you've ever dreamed or imagined." Wow. My eyes filled with tears of wonder.

The sunset followed me all the way home even until I parked my truck. I got out, stood there a moment, drinking it in one last time. The moment ended, but one day it never will.

Untangling the Knots

I took the day off today, after an extremely busy weekend. I needed it, too. I did a wedding for a couple in our church Friday night, after a Thursday night rehearsal. Saturday we spent trying to fix several problems around the house, not the least of which has been a short somewhere in our electrical system that keeps tripping a breaker to about 4 sets of lights on our main floor. My dad came up to help, and we spent much of the day trying to trace down the problem, taking apart fixture after fixture, as well as outlets. We never found the problem, even with Lisa's dad's help on Sunday afternoon. It's driving me up the wall.
On top of this, Kelsey's Homecoming game & dance were this weekend, which meant she and her girlfriends were in and out Friday & Saturday, getting ready, taking pictures, etc. That all was fun, actually- a welcome, although hectic, break from electrical problems! All their group pictures with dates were taken here, so

there were over 12 cars in our driveway at one point. Ansley stayed busy as well, with a friend of hers up from south Georgia both days.

With all that, plus my Sunday morning duties, it was an exhausting weekend.

Thankfully, the weather was great today, so I layered up and took off on a moto ride. I love this time of year, when the temps are cooler, the leaves are beginning to change, and I can go ride under clear, crisp, sunny days. I rode some back roads down to Watkinsville, got a late lunch at a chicken place I know of, then visited the local Ducati shop I enjoy stopping in on occasionally. I finally pulled back home around 4pm, a little chilly but very refreshed.

Nothing like a good, extended ride on my bike to "untangle the knots." I thanked God for the relationships with both sides of our family, for the memories we are still making with our girls, and for a nice, cozy roof over our head, even if it seems we are always working on something! And yet I am thankful for the quiet moments, the times of solitude that help me reconnect with my heart, and the heart of God. Rolling down a road at 50-60 mph on a wide-open motorcycle may not seem relaxing to many, but to those who ride, in a hard-to-explain way, it is. And I'm thankful for those few moments I have. God meets me there, and I am refreshed and renewed.

Old Hawk

Yesterday I rode down to Watkinsville, to test-ride a cool bike I saw at a motorcycle shop down there. For some time now, I've gotten the itch for another motorcycle- not getting rid of my Royal Star (I love that bike), but a 2nd bike. I've wanted a small sport/street bike, something small & lightweight, just to knock around town & ride the back roads locally. I've looked at the Ducati Monster 620, Kawasaki Ninja 500, and the Yamaha FZ6. Not a new one, but a few years old. I don't really have the $$ for one now, but hopefully in a couple of years I'll be able to.

Anyway, I had ridden down to this shop last week (see prev. post), and saw a used bike there I had never seen before- a 1989 Honda Hawk 650. I was smitten with it- one of the coolest looking little bikes I've seen in a long time! And being that old, they are really cheap to come by. I spent the past week studying them on the web, and decided I had to ride this only one I found anywhere local. It did not disappoint! I rode it a few miles, and although it's an entirely different ride than my big bike, it was a lot of fun, and very easy to handle. I thanked the moto-shop guys, and headed for home.

On the way back north, I began to think about the experience. I asked God if it be His will, when the time was right and the $$ were available, I'd love to have one. Then a Bible verse popped into my head- "Godliness with contentment is great gain." I prayed, "Father, I really love this bike you've given me to enjoy for so many years & miles now. It definitely has been a gift from you. If another bike ever comes, I will thank you. If not, I will thank you. I have been blessed more than I deserve, in every area of my life."

So often, we think God is not interested in our happiness & pleasure. "My God will supply all of your needs,..." And yet, He gives us the ability to enjoy, and so much to enjoy, in this life. He is joy, and desires we live in joy. He does often give us our wants, within His will for our lives. Yet I think sometimes I want more than I should want. Giving us joy and pleasure must be balanced against contentment. And with all He blesses me with, every day of my life, I certainly have much to be joyful about, and much to be content with.

"Godliness with contentment is great gain." *1 Timothy 6:6*

In The Storms

It's been said of bikers, "the urge to ride can overwhelm reason." Well, that was true of me today. My bike had been in the shop for almost 10 days, so when I got it back Saturday, I took the long way home. Sunday, after church, I had to meet Lisa & the girls down at the lake for Kelsey's and my niece Tori's family graduation party. They had left earlier in the morning, but I didn't get on the road until almost 1:30pm. I love the ride through the countryside to Lake Oconee, and despite the threat of thunderstorms, I went against sound judgment and took off on my bike.

I was in and out of rain within the first 10 miles. Stopping to get my rain gear on at a gas station, I rode on, storms all around me. The sky was dark, there were thunderheads that looked miles high, and sheets of rain split by lightning, on all sides it seemed. I was honestly a little unnerved, wishing I had taken 4 wheels instead of 2. As I rode, hoping to dodge as many bursts as possible, I was grumbling, complaining, bad words floating around in my head. As I got south of Bostwick, my bike began to sputter & skip, like water was affecting the plugs firing or something. I thought, "Oh great, I'll stall out in the middle of nowhere, with no cell service, and no shelter from the driving rain." But the bike kept chugging on, albeit in protest. South of Madison, I finally prayed, "God, why don't you stop the storms from hitting me for awhile??" To which I felt Him reply, "Why don't you learn to praise Me in the storms??" That struck like a lightning bolt to my soul. I rode on, contemplating what He spoke. As I thought about the situation I was in, with all this awesome, fearful wonder on display all around me, I felt very ungrateful, untrusting, and self-centered. The God who had given me life, given me new life, given me all I've ever needed for life, was telling me to enjoy Him, trust Him, praise Him in the storms. Its easy for me to ride and worship when the weather is beautiful- Why can't I ride and worship when the weather is not so beautiful?

Then I thought back on all the times in my life when things have went well for me. Its easy to love, to worship, to trust in God then. But all too often, when adversity hits, when difficulties and trials surround me, I find myself grumbling, complaining, inwardly letting the bad words float around in my head, forgetting the God who gives the good days is also the Lord of the bad days. Like the song by Casting Crowns, I need to learn to "praise You in the storm."

I had to ride back this evening the same way, dodging storms and occasionally getting pelted with heavy rain. But my perspective was different. As I rode toward thunderheads filled with darkness, driving rain, and lightning, I chose this time to follow the example of Paul & Silas in prison in Acts 16:25, and began to sing praises to God. As a storm would loom in front of me, I lifted up a song on the road, and pressed forward.

By the time I arrived home, I had only been in one heavy shower on the return trip, and God had caused me to literally dodge every other. Amazing. But whether I had been in storms or not, God had gripped me with the need to trust and not fear, to praise and not complain, to focus on Him and not on my plight.

A Heavenly perspective changes everything. He doesn't promise to clear the storms out in front of us, but He does promise to get us through them, and be with us in the midst of them. Ours is to trust and praise.

Humbling Encounters

Today was an absolutely beautiful day for March. Sunny, wispy clouds overhead, temps in the upper 60s. I rode the motorbike to the office, praying and worshiping as I rode in. I had three amazing encounters during the day that reminded me of the nearness of God. As I finished breakfast, I glanced out to our backyard, and saw four deer, grazing on our grass, with the sun rising through the woods behind them. I whispered, "Thank you Father, for this morning gift", and loaded up for work.

I came home during lunch to check on the dogs, and enjoyed a leisurely walk down our long driveway with them. The sun was bright and warm, a slight breeze was wafting through the trees, and I savored the moments before once again saddling up to go back to the office. As I rolled to the end of the driveway on the bike, I noticed a large red tail hawk right in front of me, perched on a telephone line over our mailbox. I stopped, watching to see what he would do, and he just sat there, moving his head from side to side, eye-balling me as I was him. I again whispered, "Thank you Father for this moment in time, shared with this exquisite creature you have made!" As I rode off, he remained, watching me pull away.

Later this evening, as I talked on the phone with my friend Aaron, I heard something unusual outside, so I walked out into the moon-lit driveway. I heard in the pines over my head the tell-tale "whoo-whoo, whoo-whoo, whoo" of not one, but three owls, calling to each other across the trees. Transfixed, I held my phone up for Aaron to hear, which he could, but barely. To my naked ear, they were up close and personal, almost right above me. It was awe-inspiring. I told Aaron I'd have to call him back, and I spent the next ten minutes, standing out front, under the moon and trees, listening to these three owls make music to my ears. Even the dogs sat in silence, looking skyward, listening as well. Again I whispered, "Thank you Father, for another indescribable gift tonight. I love you."

Life has become so busy it seems, and I have become so distracted, I have begun to lose sight of the little "hints of Heaven, glimpses of glory" God has placed throughout His creation, all around me. Even when I'm riding my motorcycle, which has always been a personal retreat on wheels for me, I've begun to focus on riding techniques I've been studying, practicing cornering, shifting, etc., all good things. Today reminded me to drink in the scenery all around, to get my "head on a swivel, eyes outside the cockpit" to use a fighter pilot phrase, and enjoy God in His creation again.

As we finish up our "Wonderful Outlaw" series in RockiTown this Sunday, getting to know the incredible personality of Jesus, I will communicate that we must return to simply loving Jesus- in worship, in His Word, and in His world. To quote John Eldredge from the book we based our series on, "I am making a practice of loving Jesus. Loving him for who he really is. The Jesus who gave us the oceans and rivers. Who gave us laughter. Who served up 908 bottles of wine to Cana."

And who gave me four deer, three owls, one hawk, and a couple of four-legged furry companions to enjoy it all with today.

Birds of a Feather

This past Sunday, I had a couple of amazing animal encounters again. With spring in the air, and considering my previous entry, these were pretty incredible.

After returning from church, I changed out of my "Sunday"

clothes, and took the dogs for a walk up and down the driveway. I had left the door to the den open, to let some fresh air in. As we stepped back inside, I noticed movement out of the corner of my eye. A small wren had flown into the house, and was buzzing around in the den, trying to avoid us. I chased her around the room, trying to catch her against a window, drape or something. She flew upstairs to the kitchen, right into the blinds of the breakfast nook. I gently trapped her and pulled her out, trying not to hurt the little creature. She squawked at me, very unhappy with being captured. I loosened my grip to adjust, and out she jumped, flitting around the kitchen again. She finally landed on a drape, and I was able to quickly snatch her in my hands again, still careful not to harm her.

As I walked back outside to release her, I was amazed at how tiny and fragile she was. She fit in the palm of my hand. As I opened my hands to let her go, she suddenly gripped one of my fingers with both little feet, and didn't let go. I held my hand up, this tiny bird perched now on my index finger, and she just looked at me, refusing to fly off immediately. Was she wondering why I didn't crush her, or eat her? Who knows. It couldn't have been more than 20 seconds, but she finally flew off, the dogs and I watching her departure.

Later in the afternoon, after a short nap, I was again outside with the dogs, this time sitting on the front steps, the dogs sitting on the front walkway. Birds were chirping and singing everywhere, all around us. Suddenly, in a flash, a large red-tailed hawk swooped down out of a nearby tree, and caught a small bird in his talons, tumbling into the grass not five feet from Johnny. Before any of us could even react, the hawk was off toward the woods, the little victim squeaking in its clutches. Shocking. My first thought was, could this have been the same little wren I released earlier? I concluded it was not, based on the pile of grey feathers in the grass where they had landed. Still, I felt sadness for the sudden demise of the little bird, although I understand it is part of life right now. Then I wondered, was this the same hawk I encountered at the end of the driveway last week? Very likely could have been. I see and hear hawks all around our property, fairly regularly.

God has created a beautiful, wild world for us to enjoy, and sometimes, we are given the opportunity to experience it up close and personal. The little wren in my hands, the large, powerful hawk in front of me. Both display the beauty and power of our God. For now, this is a fallen world, where attack and defense, tooth and claw, are a part of life. A day is coming, however, when "the wolf will live with the lamb, the leopard will lie down with the goat, the calf and the lion and the yearling together;" and the hawk will perch on my hand, next to the wren.

5 RIDING & PRAYING

On Display

We've had beautiful weather the past couple of days, so I decided to hop on my motorbike and ride the back roads before dark. There were plenty of other bikers doing the same thing, and it was a great ride- cool, crisp temps, deserted roads, woods & pasturelands, and a great sunset for the ride toward home. As I rode, taking it all in and savoring the moment, I thanked the God who created it all. Then it occurred to me- of all the things our Father is (holy, just, loving, etc.), He is also the ultimate Artist. Creation is His ever-changing canvas, and His creativity is seen in everything from a breath-taking sunset to a ladybug that lands on my windshield at a stop sign. Artwork always says something about its artist, and certainly all creation says much about our Creator/Father. Spend some time enjoying Him in His masterpiece soon- its always on display!

"The heavens declare the glory of God,...the earth is full of His glory..."

His Workmanship

Just an added thought to the previous entry:
As I thought about it today, an amazing thought came to me. With all the wonder God has designed into His creation, as vast as the farthest galaxy and as tiny as the smallest cell, He considers you and I the crowning achievement of His creative masterpiece. We each are "fearfully and wonderfully made", as David wrote in Psalms, and His most beloved creatures. We are created in His image, and He loves us more than all else in the universe.
To me, this is very comforting, assuring. As we enjoy His masterful creation, we can enjoy the One who so enjoys us. And His heart is always toward us.
"For we are His workmanship, created in Christ Jesus for good works..." Ephesians 2:10

Obedience

Last week I took a few days off to spend with my wife & girls, and with my parents at their Oconee lake house. Great place to relax and unwind. In fact the ride down there, through the farm & dairy country, is as pleasant as the destination!
I rode my motorcycle down, praying and worshipping God, as I often do while riding. About halfway there, passing through Bostwick, GA, I just asked God, "Father, what would you speak to my heart about? What would you teach me out here?" What ensued was a heart conversation with God that was both simple and profound.
What He brought to my mind was obedience. I prayed, "Why do we often not like the concept of obeying You? We want to focus on Your love, Your grace, enjoying Your blessings in our lives...Yet our rebellious nature wants to resist obedience sometimes. I know you're not some cosmic dictator, demanding our fearful

allegiance. Why obedience?"

Then He spoke into my heart- "Why do you want your children to obey you?"

I thought, then replied, "Because I love them, and want what's best for them."

"Go on," He whispered.

"Well, I also want to keep them from harm, from danger."

He pressed me further. "What else?"

"I want them to grow into responsible, mature, caring adults," I said.

"Anything else?" God spoke.

"Yes, actually. I want us to live and love in harmony under our roof. To really be a close, loving family," I said.

God then spoke to my heart, "If you desire all these things for your girls, how much more do you think I desire these for all My children? Those are also My motivations for your obedience."

I reflected on that the rest of the week- not only on this simple yet amazing conversation with the Father, but on the real meaning and purpose of obedience. It boils down to love- God's motivation in all His dealings with us. And I love Him all the more for it.

"You must live as obedient children. Don't slip back into your old ways of living to satisfy your own desires. You didn't know any better then. But now you must be holy in everything you do, just as God chose you to be holy. For the Scriptures say, 'You must be holy, because I am holy.'" 1 Peter 1:14-16

A Father's Watchcare

Yesterday I began my work week the way I do every day- breakfast and some time in God's Word. Unsure where to begin, I simply prayed, "Father, what would you have me read?" I felt the gentle impression, "Psalm 91." As I turned there, I remembered that my mom & dad pray verse 11 every time they ride their motorcycle, and they pray that for me as well. In fact, I pray that verse now myself!

Anyway, I read the whole chapter (its not that long), but kept coming back to the first verse-

"He who dwells in the shelter of the Most High will abide in the shadow of the Almighty."

I found myself contemplating that verse the rest of the day, and returned to it this morning. Why this verse? And what is it saying to me? I began to break down the meaning of the words in it, and this is what it spoke to me-

"The one who fully lives under the covering and safety of the Father, will stay intimately connected and protected under the shadow of His presence."

The image of being a little kid, holding the hand of my dad, walking and talking together, his shadow shielding me from the sun, and feeling secure in his presence, came to mind in this verse and its meaning. I felt this same presence and assurance, only deeper, in my soul, with God this morning. My Father is still watching over me, still covering me, still walking with me, even though I so often, like a little kid, want to squirm away and run to other things. Yet deep in my heart, my desire is to dwell in His shelter, abide in His shadow. May that be the definition and direction of my life.

Being, Not Doing

I've been reading John Eldredge's book, *Walking With God.* In one of the sections, he challenges the reader to ask God 2 questions-
Lord, how do I think I am doing?
Lord, how do you think I am doing?

So often, his point was, how we see ourselves is vastly different than the way God sees us, and wants us to see ourselves.

Anyway, I asked God those 2 questions, and kept getting distracted every morning, so I kept returning to those questions for several days. When you ask God a question, He will answer, in His time, in His way. Stay with Him.

Last Friday I went for a motorcycle ride (as I often do), and God spoke to me while riding (as He often does). John had written the phrase that came to describe his answer to the 1st question was, "Just barely", and that's how I've felt. Just barely doing well, as a husband, a father, a friend, a minister, a child of God. So easily distracted, so easily tripped up. "Just barely" fit how I saw myself. Riding some back road outside Rutledge, Ga., God spoke to my heart, "You are mine, and you are loved." He continued- "That was the wrong question for you. It's not about doing, it's about being. Its not about performance, it's about position. You are mine, and you are loved." Simple truth, I've known these for years, but it was so good hearing from my Father personally on this. My position is secure, as His beloved son. The "being" is just that- Being in His hands, in His presence, in His plan. The doing grows out of the being.

That night, I found myself in Jeremiah 31:3- "I have loved you with an everlasting love; therefore I have drawn you with loving-kindness."

Disruptions

It's funny how we so often work so hard to arrange for our own happiness. And funny how often life happens, and disrupts our "best laid plans of man."

I had planned out my Saturday perfectly- Ansley & Kelsey both had responsibilities all day, so I planned to get up around 9:30am, eat breakfast, then join Lisa in some fun yard work with flower planting, opening our flower garden fountain, etc. After lunch, I planned to take a good, long solo motorcycle ride, be back for dinner, then settle down to make my final prep for Sunday morning kid's church.

That was my plan- and it didn't take long before it was disrupted. Kelsey had been run off the road in her car by a "hit & run" truck a couple of days before, and along with car body damage, she had blown a tire. After getting a spare on it, yesterday she used Lisa's car to visit a friend, and promptly took a nail puncture in one of those tires! So my Saturday afternoon would be spent at a tire store, replacing two tires for two cars. Not what I had planned...

I was down in the dumps, thinking a perfect day was lost. My plans were ruined. Fortunately, God got my attention. He reminded me that my attempt to arrange for my own happiness was not the point. My life was in His hands, and He would provide for all my needs.

As it turns out, the tires were both fixed quickly and without a huge cost, as they were still under warranty on both cars. I ended up returning home by 5pm, and Lisa said, "Hey, it's been a trying day. Go take a ride." So I took off, and had a wonderful, beautiful, relaxing ride as the sun slowly began to set. I rode to Good Hope and back, just letting the road and wind and scenery untangle my mind.

On a back road, by a postcard perfect scene overlooking a sun setting behind a farm on rolling hills, I looked up, and saw a break in the gathering clouds. The hole in the cloud took the shape of a heart, and God spoke into mine- "Just a little reminder of My love for you." I replied, "Thank you Father, I love you too." He had reminded me not only of His love, but also that life's purpose and pleasures were in His hands. I so easily complain about what I don't have, or what doesn't go according to my plans, then I realize I have been blessed with so very much, and I would not have had my life turn out any other way. I among men, am most blessed, more than I deserve.

I Delight in You

I took a ride Friday morning down to my parent's lake house on Oconee, for a home-cooked lunch from my mom, and a little moto-maintenance help from my dad. The ride down was, well, as close to heaven as I've felt in some time. Perfect riding conditions- cool temps, warm sun, gentle breeze, the world in full bloom, wide-open roads. The kind of morning that you want to freeze in time, and linger therein. In all, almost 2 hours of biker bliss!
As I often do while riding, I worship and pray. I'm totally focused- on the road ahead, the bike beneath me, the world around me, and my Lord over me. I prayed for family & friends, I worshiped & praised for all the beauty in His world surrounding me, and I asked that He speak into my heart whatever He wanted to say to me. At one point, between Bostwick and Madison, I prayed, "Father, do I bring You pleasure? I want You to be proud of me." I felt His voice speak into my heart, "I am greatly pleased with you. I take great delight in you." It thrilled my heart, and I quickly replied, "Show me how I can bring You greater pleasure!" No sooner had those words crossed my mind, when He pretty much cut off my thought process with this truth- "You can't bring me anymore pleasure than you already do. I am fully pleased with you. I delight in you, not because of anything you do, but because you are Mine." I let the weight of that truth sink in, but still I responded, "Even with my faults and shortcomings? I struggle with my thought life, my tongue, my distractedness, my feelings of failure at home...I sometimes don't feel like I bring You much pleasure." To which He stated, "It doesn't matter. My pleasure in you is not based on

what you do. It's based on My love for you. I delight in you."

I rode on the rest of the way, just letting that simple but profound truth settle into my heart. I knew it I think, I just needed Him to remind of me of it again. We let so many of the world's cares, fears, and sins burden us down, that we forget the great love of God for us, which we cannot earn, nor can we lose. Sometimes, we just need to unplug from the world and pull aside for a time, and let Him begin to speak again. I'll live for Him, not because I need to bring Him pleasure, but because He already is pleased with me.

6 MINISTRY MUSINGS

Prison

Sunday night our motorcycle group went to prison! We joined
Terry Buice of Barnabas Prison Ministry at Gwinnett Prison to help
conduct a worship service for the inmates. Terry works in several
prisons full-time, counseling and assisting inmates in many ways.
We go in with him on Sunday nights from time to time to help
with worship services. After some spirited music and singing
(hearing a room full of inmates singing hymns and songs to God is
amazing), I got to preach, and I talked on Real Freedom in Christ:
getting free from the sins that imprison and enslave us. After I
finished, 5 men wanted to place their faith in Jesus Christ, several
more wanted prayer for struggles in their lives, and 4 were getting
ready to go home by the end of the month, so we prayed over
them, for their paths to continue with God. In all, it was an
amazing, Spirit-filled night. So often, like those inmates, people

must hit rock-bottom from their own bad choices before they look to the God who loves them and can redeem their lives. I find that in many of those men, and too little out here in the "free world." We get imprisoned by so many things in our lives- the only real freedom comes from knowing and living with the One who created, knows, and loves us.

"If the Son has set you free, then you are truly free." –Jesus

The Moving Wall

This past week our Hebron motorcycle group had the privilege of escorting the Moving Wall to Dacula. The Wall is a traveling half-scale replica of the Vietnam Memorial in Washington DC, making its way across the country. Hebron hosted it this weekend out on our property facing the post office. We were invited to ride with CMA in a motorcycle escort of the memorial from Lawrenceville to our town. We rode in formation behind its transport truck, carrying it all the way out 316 to Dacula, with full police escort out front and behind. It was a tremendous honor to participate in the motorcade, and an honor to help others remember our veterans and their fallen comrades from the war. We had a total of 18 bikes in the motorcade, joining 5 police motorcycles and 2 police cars. It was an event I'll always remember.

Honoring the Fallen

Last weekend I got to participate in something that was a huge honor for me. Hebron Baptist hosted the funeral for Lance Cpl. Stephen Johnson, the son of two beloved members of our church, killed in action by an IED in Iraq. The Spirit Riders motorcycle group was invited to participate in the funeral procession, along with members of CMA and a group called the Patriot Guard Riders. These bikers are a group from across America that attend the funerals of fallen soldiers, to honor them with color guards, and to insure any protestors don't show up and get close enough to disturb and disrespect the family.

We rode at the beginning of the funeral procession to the cemetery, and provided flags at both the church and the cemetery. This was a great honor for all of us involved, and humbling to have been invited by the family to participate. Whatever anyone may feel about the wars in Iraq and Afghanistan, our young men and women are there fighting terror for us and the people of those countries, so we won't have to fight them here in our own backyard. For that, we owe Stephen Johnson and all our armed forces a debt of gratitude.

Acts of Kindness

Today I received a letter from a couple who last year at this time lost a son in Iraq. The letter told of how much my being there with them in their time of uncertainty over his initial MIA status, then when he was found dead, had meant to the family. Enclosed was also a substantial monetary gift they wanted me to have. They wrote, "The time you spent reaching out to us, caring for us, just being there for our family, meant more to us than you know. We will never forget you."

Sadly, I had forgotten them in the past year. I recalled the night when, while I was the weekend hospital/emergency pastor, I had responded to a call to visit the house of a new couple in the church, whose son was missing in action in Iraq. I spent a couple of hours with the family, who consisted of the mom, dad, and two sisters, one of which was married with two kids in our children's ministry. As I saw the fear and grief they had, I felt compelled to keep going by their house that weekend, and on into the next week, until the word came that the son's body had been found.

I had helped in some minor details of the funeral, and had been invited to ride in the motorcycle escort of the funeral, which was a great honor. I kept in touch with the family only occasionally over the later months, then it gradually faded from my memory- until today.

Amazing what small gestures and acts of kindness can actually mean in someone else's life. What I saw as just doing my duty, had in reality made a huge impact on this family in their time of pain. One of my daughters told me, "I guess you never know how far one nice thing can go for somebody." So true.

I remember being on the receiving end myself once, as an 8th grader 30+ years ago. I had been lumped in with a bullying bunch of boys that year, with none of my friends in classes, lunch, PE, etc. It was the worst year of my life, to this day. Constant cruelty, humiliation, pain, at the hands of these punks- I was the easy target, being the smallest in the class that year.

One day, sitting alone at lunch (as usual), Laurel, one of the popular girls in the 8th grade, left her table, then came and sat with me. I don't remember all she said, but I recall this: "You're different than the other guys. I like that about you. Don't worry about them, they're all jerks. I like you just the way you are." That simple act of kindness, those simple words, spoken by that beautiful little blond, changed the course of that year for me- and I guess changed my life. I'm 44 years old, and I still recall them, and recall every detail of that moment, to this day. And I will be forever grateful.

I've heard a phrase- "Practice random acts of kindness." That's a great rule to live by. In fact, that's being the hands and feet and words of Jesus to people, as I heard a guy say once. Something our world needs more of.

Random Acts of Christmas

I had hospital visitation duty earlier this week, here right before the holidays. I usually don't mind the duty, in fact I somewhat enjoy it- being an encouragement to people, being out on the road on my bike, out of the office. This on-call rotation was difficult for me, though. It wasn't the miles or the number of hospitals our people were in- although covering about 250 miles between about a dozen hospitals in two days was exhausting! What made it difficult were the people I visited. To name a few, there was a teenager who had been hit by a car while waiting to catch the bus to school, in ICU on a ventilator with probable brain damage; a smiling 3 year old boy with anxious parents, waiting on test results to find out if their son has cystic fibrosis or not; a 50-something man who had undergone his 2nd heart bypass surgery, and was lonely and discouraged. But the most difficult for me was a lady I visited up in Gainesville, who is slowly dying. I had visited her last month, and she was up sitting in her chair in the hospital room, smiling & happy. We talked, laughed, prayed together, and I just had a great visit with her. This time I came to see her, she was on life support, tubes and IV's running all over her, and she was comatose, unresponsive with eyes half opened. I was shocked and saddened. I spoke to her and prayed over her anyway, in case she could hear anything at all. She is only 11 years older than me, and likely will not see the new year.

It was a sobering couple of days, and I really have not talked about it much. I guess I am reminded that, in the midst of the wonder and fanfare of the Christmas season, even with the hope that the birth of our Savior brings, we still live in a world of suffering and pain, and this will be a sad, painful Christmas for many, and for those they love. All the more reason to look for opportunities to commit "Random Acts of Christmas", as our church is emphasizing this holiday.

Following the Reason for the Season,

Revival Behind Bars

Tonight I rode with the Spirit Riders to join Chaplain Terry Buice for a service with the inmates of I. W. Davis Prison up in Jefferson. I didn't really feel like going, but I'm glad I did. We rode up to Jefferson, ate at Mike's Grill, then on to the prison. We were joined there by Terry and the pastor & members of Martin Baptist Church. Little did we know what would happen this evening.

We greeted each inmate as he came in the meeting room, as the small Martin choir warmed up. When all the inmates were in, about 60 in all, the choir began with 3 songs they had prepared. The inmates sat quietly, listening, until the choir leader invited the men to join them in a few songs. We sang "I'll Fly Away", "Amazing Grace", and a couple of others. The inmates began to sing louder and louder, totally throwing themselves into the worship. The Martin pastor spoke on Philippians 3, having a passion for Christ instead of the things that drag us down. Terry concluded by giving men an opportunity to come forward to give their lives to Christ, and 17 men walked to the front. We each took a few of them and helped them trust Christ, and it was a precious time, praying with each of these men.

Terry had prepared a portable baptism pool out in the yard, and as the last of the sun's light left the sky, the Spirit Riders, the church group, and the inmates gathered around as we baptized all 17 right then and there. I got to baptize several myself, which was a huge honor for me. Everyone clapped and cheered for each man as he came up out of the water, and when we were all done, we gathered around them all, laid hands on them, and prayed over them. We concluded out in the yard, in the dark by now, singing "Amazing Grace" one last time. Amid hugs and handshakes, the inmates filed back to their dorms, and we readied for home, riding back by the light of a full moon.

Terry had informed us earlier that the state was closing this prison, and within a month all these inmates would be sent to other institutions across the state. That knowledge made what happened there tonight all the more special. We really experienced God's Spirit & love tonight, and our prayer is that the men of I. W. Davis will carry this not only to wherever they go next, but the rest of their lives. May they go on and walk with Christ, all the days of their lives.

"I am confident of this very thing, that He who began a good work in you will carry it to completion until the day of Christ Jesus." Philippians 1:6

9-11 Ride to Remember

Today I had the great honor of participating in two 9-11 memorial services, as a chaplain & speaker. I was invited by the Red Knights motorcycle club, made up of fire fighters, to ride along with them in their annual "Ride to Remember 9-11" motorcycle event, and speak at ceremonies in Lawrenceville's Gwinnett Justice bldg & the GPSTC in Forsyth.

Several of the Spirit Riders rode with me, and the Gwinnett event featured color guards from the police & fire depts, and short speeches by the Gwinnett fire marshal & myself. It was very humbling for me to speak and participate in this, made more meaningful by the presence of the mother of Lcpl Stephen Johnston, USMC, killed in Iraq in Oct. 2006. The Johnston family are Hebron members, and I spent much time with them when they got word of Stephen's death 2 years ago. Mrs. Johnston came up to me before the ceremony, and handed me a camo bandana with Psalm 91 printed on it, saying, "This was one of his bandanas, that he would wear under his helmet. We would like you to carry it with you today in the ceremonies and on the ride.

You can wear it under your helmet too, if you like." It deeply moved me, and I told the audience about Stephen in my message. And I wore the bandana under my helmet.

35 bikes saddled up and rode in the HOV lane down I-85 to Clayton Harley Davidson for a break, then on to Forsyth.

*A funny aside- at about 11:55am, I and two of our guys went back inside the H-D building for a quick sip of coffee, only to come back out to an empty lot- they'd left without us, no warning! We took off on I-75 south, blasting down the interstate to catch up. We caught them all 20 min. down the road, and fell back in formation. Imagine that- they left behind one of their keynote speakers!!

The ceremony at the Georgia Public Safety Training Center in Forsyth was similar, with a fire dept. color guard, a fire service speaker, and myself. At both ceremonies, I related how, in the same way our public servants put themselves in harm's way to rescue, liberate, and protect our people, Jesus Christ entered a world in turmoil & chaos to save us from sin & evil, self-sacrificially.

A very solemn and reverent event, in both places.

We rode back up country roads, through Monticello, Mansfield, Social Circle, and Monroe. The weather was cool & partly sunny, the surrounding countryside both calming & breathtaking. The perfect way to conclude a wonderful, tiring, humbling, day of remembrance & reflection.

May we never forget- the sacrifices of our public servants, and ultimately, our Savior Jesus Christ.

Tony

Since I joined Facebook last September, I've reconnected with many old high school and college friends. Its been like an internet reunion! Most recently, I found another high school friend named Tony, who I haven't heard from since we graduated. Come to find out, he and his family have been missionaries in a large city in Mexico for a number of years.

I was on Facebook late one night this past weekend, when he popped up on the IM feature, to say hi. Wow, I thought, its Tony, down in Mexico right now! Ah, the wonders of modern technology...

We "conversed" for the better part of an hour, catching up with each other's family and ministry. As we dialogued, I found he works among the poorest of poor in the city, meeting people where they are and meeting their needs with the love of Christ. He said we are in similar situations, serving those the world and the church often neglect or at least don't prioritize. I told him I thought the work he does is much more heart-breaking and emotionally draining than what I do. He sees so much pain, illness, poverty and wickedness down there, I can't even conceive of.

I told him I would pray for him, his family and his work. And I plan to keep my word.

I found his blog online, and his last two entries were about faith & doubt. He struggles, as we all do at times, with questions- what am I doing down here? Am I really making a difference? Did God really call me to this? Is He with me? Am I really doing His will? Then he understands, as I so often come back to, that "we walk by faith, and not by sight." As we keep walking, keep working, God keeps leading, He keeps using us, to further His Kingdom. And He confirms it in our hearts, in the little things day to day, in His Word, and in our hearts.

The solution to doubts? Keep walking.

Now, when I get down on myself, or get selfish or self-centered, I think of Tony, serving Christ down on the streets of a city in Mexico, devoting his life to serving Christ by serving "the least of these." May I so honor Christ in my own life and ministry.

In The Flesh

I read an amazing article in the latest edition of "HomeLife" magazine, of all places. Entitled "In the Flesh" by Scottish writer Christian George, it addresses the astonishing truth of God in human form, Jesus Christ, in a new and refreshing way. The article had my attention from the opening lines-

"Let's get right down to business. Jesus took off His clothes. From the beginning of time, He planned to trade heavenly silk for soiled humanity...What a thought! That God would feel the fever of an infection and the throb of a headache... God stripped Himself that we might be clothed."

I don't think we fully appreciate the stupendous declaration found in John 1:14- "The Word became flesh and made His dwelling among us." We miss the utter vulgarity & seeming absurdity of deity setting aside glory and trading it all for dirty humanity. As George further explains, "Jesus knew pain firsthand. He was not an airbrushed model who never knew a wart or wrinkle. No, God became real blood and real bone."

Last Sunday night, Pastor Kevin explored this further in his sermon. Addressing the heights and depths of deity putting on humanity, he began by pointing out where Jesus came from. Reading from Isaiah 6:1-4, he "pulled back the veil" so to speak, revealing the incomprehensible glory and majesty Jesus came to us from. A massive throne, the Lord seated on it, His robe filling the temple, with 6-winged creatures flying about Him, shouting His praise, His glory like smoke filling the chamber, and His voice shaking the foundations. It reminded me of a similar scene that John saw and recorded in Revelation 4:1-11. That passage defies description. To read it and try to imagine it is beyond comprehension. A description would fail here. Go read it.

And yet Jesus left all that to put on human skin, and start off a helpless human baby. The Jews were looking for a military messiah, who would rescue them from the Romans and restore the kingdom of David, making them a world power again. Instead, God did just the opposite. Jesus became a man from a dirt-poor little town, who never traveled farther than 100 miles from His birth home, and was mocked, ridiculed, spit on, beaten, and rejected by those He came to save. "How odd of God!" George exclaims in his article. And yet as he points out, Jesus understands what it's like to be in our skin. "He knew the agony, numbness, and intensity of being human. No other 'god' took so radical a jump as Jesus... The incarnation (literally 'into flesh') is unique to Christianity because the kamikaze Christ plunged into death so that we might have life. Because Jesus was man, God identifies with us. Because Jesus was divine, we identify with God."

I found myself in Isaiah 53 a couple of days ago in my morning quiet time. The passage describes the complete degradation and humiliation the Christ would endure for fallen humanity. When I read it all, and thought back over the Isaiah 6 and Revelation 4 chapters, I was dumbfounded at the "furious love of God" for us, as Rich Mullins used to describe it. That Jesus would leave all that He left behind (creatures specifically created to constantly worship Him, for pete's sake!) to walk among us and endure what He did at our hands, all to restore us to a right relationship to the Father- leaves me speechless before Him. My praise and worship seems so inadequate.

Yet I will praise Him, with my words and my works- this upcoming holiday season, the rest of my life, and all eternity. "My utmost, for His highest."

Solomon's Legacy

I was reading this morning in 1 Kings 11, about King Solomon's final years. It was a sobering read, to be truthful. When people typically think of Solomon, they usually recall the following facts about him- his father was King David, the greatest king in Israel's history; he succeeded his father to the throne; Solomon was offered anything his heart would desire by God, and he (wisely) chose wisdom to lead; as a result, God gave him unsurpassed wisdom, but also blessed him with vast wealth, power, and influence across the world. What fantastic potential and promise! Solomon penned most of the Proverbs, some of the Psalms are attributed to him, and scholars believe he wrote Ecclesiastes and Song of Songs as well. Solomon was given the privilege of constructing the first great Temple, built up Jerusalem as well as other great projects across the country, constructed a vast navy to sail the Mediterranean, the Red Sea, and beyond. His wisdom, fame, and wealth were beyond any of his time. All because he started well- he dedicated himself to follow God, to walk humbly before Him, and to lead God's people with wisdom and compassion.

But something happened along the way. By chapter 11, Solomon began to waver and weaken.

His wealth, power and fame began to go to his head, as he accumulated more and more for himself, and began to treat his people as servants rather than God's people, taxing them heavily and pressing them into slave labor. He gathered for himself literally hundreds of wives and concubines, to feed his lusts. And he allowed for the worship of false gods among all his wives, and ultimately among the people, eventually participating himself. In short, rather growing into a wise old man, he became an old fool. The sad final years of his life can be summed up in these verses- "Now the Lord was angry with Solomon because his heart was turned away from the Lord,... he did not observe what the Lord had commanded."(v.9-10) In fact, his final recorded act as king was a plot to kill the man God was going to give part of his kingdom to upon his death. He fought against God while at the very end of his life!

His story startled and shook me. I had not looked at Solomon this way before. He did not finish well, but in shame.

I hopped on my bike and rode to work, enjoying the cool, clear morning, but praying that God would protect and preserve my heart, wholly for Him. I never want to make choices that would bring shame upon myself, my family, my people, my church, and ultimately, my God. I want to finish well, finish strong, and leave a legacy of love for God, love for people, and love for life. I want to hear God say, "Well done, welcome home!", not "What were you thinking?!" I know I'll not be perfect, I'll make mistakes sometimes, but may I never destroy God's work in and through me. May my life, overall, bring Him glory and honor.

May my epitaph one day read- "He walked with God, and brought others along."

A Hero

A couple of years ago, I wrote about an old high school friend who serves as a missionary/church planter/orphanage director in the North Mexico city of Matamoros. We reconnected on Facebook, and have been corresponding ever since. Tony and his family have been there for a number of years, laboring under difficult circumstances to reach people for Christ and improve the lives of the people in that city. They have sacrificed so much in the name of the Gospel, and they count it all joy.

Back in high school, Tony's nickname was "Mumbley" by his friends. He was shy and quiet, didn't talk much, but when he did, he had this deep, low voice and southern drawl. And he always had a smile on his face. Hard not to like him. I never would have pictured Tony as a preacher/teacher, and a missionary in a foreign land.

But Tony is my hero.

Over the past 4 years, around 30,000 people have died in Mexico in the drug wars between the cartels, the Mexican police & military, and innocent civilians. It truly is a war zone down there, along the border between the U.S. and Mexico. Whether you are for or against amnesty for illegal immigrants here in the U.S., it's hard for us to imagine the hellish nightmare and fear people live under down there every day. Little wonder so many want to flee across the border.

Tony lives and serves right in the middle of all this in Matamoros. He sees not only poverty, disease, and despair daily, but he also witnesses the crime, the death, the destruction of the drug war. Mexico is a country suffering a slow, painful death, and Tony is right there, reaching out to those in need, touching one heart at a time with the love of Christ. He sometimes sends out messages to us back here in the States, simply asking, "pray for peace in Mexico" and "pray hearts will turn to Christ, the only hope for Mexico."

Sometimes when I reflect on the fears we face back home here, I think of the uncertain economy, rising prices, rising taxes, job loss, healthcare issues, and so on. All very real concerns, no doubt. Then I'll get a message from Tony, and I'm reminded of how he, his family, and those they minister among fear for their lives, daily. Sobering thought.

And so I pray for my friend, serving Christ by serving "the least of these", in a war-torn border town called Matamoros. May God protect him, provide for him, multiply his work, and richly reward him one day.

The Rest of the Story

I was sending off my tax stuff at the Post Office earlier this week, and a young mom with 2 small kids was in front of me. When I left, she was out at her van, putting her kids in car seats, and had her hood open. I pulled over to offer help, and she said her engine wouldn't start, wouldn't even turn over. I pulled in my truck next to her, and said, "Let me see if I can help." Turns out, her battery terminals were full of corrosion, and the negative cable popped right off. I cleaned up her battery connections, tightened everything down, and it started right up. She was very grateful, and tried to pay me $10, saying, "No one stops to help anymore, I am so thankful for you. And I don't carry a cell phone, so I didn't know what to do." I gently refused her $$, so she said, "Well, can I give you a hug at least?" which I said was fine, and said, "I'm just glad I could help. God bless you & your family." I left, as did she, but I was thinking, 'I wish I had said more, shared my faith more.' So I prayed for her and her family, that they would somehow come to faith in Christ if they did not already know Him.
Here's the Paul Harvey "Rest of the Story." I pulled into the parking lot at Hebron, and she pulled in behind me, a few spaces down! I got out, and asked her, "Are your kids in our Preschool program here?" which she said they were. When I introduced myself to her, her eyes got wide, and she exclaimed, "I'm Patricia Mason*, my husband Ben* has been playing telephone tag with you for a couple of weeks about Cade*!" (their son, for our new Christian class). We talked as she brought her kids in, and they told me they've been visiting here for awhile. I walked to my

94

office feeling overwhelmed that God had me there to help her at just that moment, and that they were a family I've been trying to connect with for some time now! Penny, one of the ladies in our business office, had been at the Post Office too, saw the whole thing, and told me later that morning, "I saw you help that young lady, and thought, 'Oh, there's Rob, doing a random act of kindness!' I guess it wasn't so random, was it??" Definitely an unexpected opportunity.

God works in mysterious ways, we've always heard. Amazingly, He'll use us to touch other's lives in "divine appointments" like this, if we will just be open and available. May I always be ready to respond to these "unexpected adventures."

*Names changed for privacy.

Jesus' Dad

I found this section in Max Lucado's great book, "In the Grip of Grace", and it bears repeating-

"Can anything make me stop loving you?" God asks. "Watch me speak your language, sleep on your earth, and feel your hurts. Behold the maker of sight and sound as he sneezes, coughs, and blows his nose. You wonder if I understand how you feel? Look into the dancing eyes of the kid in Nazareth; that's God walking to school. Ponder the toddler at Mary's table; that's God spilling his milk.

"You wonder how long my love will last? Find your answer on a splintered cross, on a craggy hill. That's me you see up there, your maker, your God, nail-stabbed and bleeding. Covered in spit and sin-soaked.

"That's your sin I'm feeling. That's your death I'm dying. That's your resurrection I'm living. That's how much I love you."

Wow. I'm stunned into worshipful silence.

I was thinking today about the tremendous, life-changing experience the birth of Christ was to His earthly dad, Joseph. Here he is, a simple construction worker in Nazareth, getting ready for his upcoming marriage to his bride-to-be, Mary. Nothing extraordinary about him- just a regular, working class guy. Then he finds out his fiancé is pregnant, obviously NOT by him! I can't imagine the horror, shock, anger, fear, and sorrow he must have felt. But being a good guy, he was just planning to break everything off quietly, try to pick up the pieces and get on with his life- until the night an angel came to him, with some incredible news...

I found that, in the book of Matthew, an angel spoke to Joseph a total of 4 times, from the first revelation that Mary was carrying the Messiah, to the final word that it was safe to go back home from Egypt. No matter what his circumstances looked like, no matter what anyone might have thought, no matter how crazy it all seemed- Joseph trusted and followed God, and reaped the benefits of helping raise up God in human flesh.

Imagine- those rough, calloused hands cradling Divinity; those worn-down fingernails tickling holy infant toes and nose; those thick arms playfully wrestling with the toddler God; stopping the cart, because his 10-year old son, who also happens to be the Lord of all the universe, wants to ride to the supply store with him. It must have been amazing almost every day to think that, "this cute little kid running around my house is the Lord God Almighty in human skin. And I'm teaching Him to fish and play ball and swing a hammer without smashing His fingers."

We don't hear anymore about Joseph after Jesus turned 12. All we know about him we find in the first few chapters of Matthew and Luke. But I know one thing- he was a man blessed by God, no doubt. And I look forward to meeting him someday, and hearing his stories about being "dad" to the Son of God. I'm sure he has some incredible stories to tell...

The Word became flesh, and made His dwelling among us. John 1:14

7 FAMILY MATTERS

The Old Man Rides Again

I was on vacation last week during Spring Break, and had a unique opportunity to do something I never have before in my life- I went motorcycle riding with my dad. We have never owned bikes at the same time over the years, and now we do. So, we made family history! We rode around Lake Oconee across 2 days, and my mom even hopped on and rode some as well. For me, it was an amazing time- out on the open country roads, in beautiful weather, riding with my old biker dad. He first began riding in 1957, on a chopped/bobbed '54 Triumph. He's owned various Triumphs over the years, but has been off bikes for about 15 years. Rebuilding and riding a little 1985 Yamaha we got from a friend of mine, and getting out on the road with me, was a memorable time. We had a great couple of days, and my mom took tons of pictures while riding on the back of my bike.

What I came away with? Savor every moment with those you

love, and make memories with them when you can- you'll carry those memories the rest of your life, long after the events and people are gone.

Birthday Surprises

Yesterday I turned 43 years old (young). I had spent the morning riding my bike and meeting my parents for lunch, and when my girls got home from school, they said they each wanted to take me out for my birthday present. I went to the mall with Ansley, then to a motorcycle shop with Kelsey. I had two great "daddy & daughter" times, in the same day! When Kels and I got back to the house, we walked in and "SURPRISE!!!" a bunch of the Children's Church leaders and families shocked me nearly to death with a birthday party! I nearly had a heart attack! Totally caught me by surprise. We ate, talked, laughed together on into the evening. What a great time it was. The older I get, the less I expect big things for birthdays (you want to forget them, if possible!), but the more I look forward to times with family and good friends. And these folks are among my very closest friends. I'm thankful for family and friends in the Lord- we'll always have each other in Him!

Father & Son Road Trip #1

I just got back from a 4-day road trip with my dad. We rode our bikes up into N. Carolina to the Blue Ridge Parkway, and rode it, the Cherohala Skyway, the Foothills Parkway, and famed "Tail of the Dragon", US 129, among other roads in NC, TN & North Ga. Four days of fun riding, breathtaking mountains & valleys, and great fellowship with my father, and our Father. Riding up there in the higher elevations of the Smoky Mountains is both awe-inspiring and dangerous. A fellow biker wiped out up on the Blue

Ridge, right after we hit the Parkway, and we were the first to come up on him and help.

The sights we saw, the experiences we had, and fellowship we enjoyed made it among the most memorable times of my life. We both found a deeper friendship as father and son, and found a deeper worship and intimacy with our Heavenly Father, up there on those roads, among those mountains. The sad part is always when the journey ends, and you must come back to civilization (such as it is!). And yet I know, from the very heart of God, that a day will come when the adventure will never end, the discoveries will never cease, the fellowship will never be broken, and the beauty will be eternal & unblemished.
"Eye has not seen, nor ear heard, nor have entered into the heart of man, what God has prepared for those who love Him..." 1 Corinthians 2:9

Family Ride

Wednesday I took the day off to do something with my parents & brothers that we never have done before- we all went for a motorcycle ride! One of my brothers flew in from TX, the other came up from Locust Grove, and they both rented bikes, then we all went for a day of riding together. We rode through towns all around Lake Oconee where my parents live, and it was an incredible time. We also stopped in Rutledge for lunch together, just the "original Brooks 5", another thing we haven't done since we were all back in school.
Yet as our day came to a close, it all ended on a sour note. I had left for my home, and my dad, mom, and brothers rode the rentals back. Mark took one bike, Rick the other, and on the way there, my dad got to ride Rick's rental some. Not far down the

road, in a tight corner, my dad lost control of the big bike, went into the dirt/pine straw in the corner, and slid out, himself flying off the bike. He sustained 2 rib fractures, 3 pelvic fractures, and ended up at Atlanta Medical Center. Amazingly, upon x-ray, his bones had all reconnected, and everything was where it was supposed to be! By Thursday p.m., the docs sent him home, saying, "There's nothing we can do for you here that you can't do for yourself- Go home!" Today, he is sore & stiff, but getting around pretty good. I told him he's like an old wild turkey- wrinkly, stubborn, and tough. He even plans to get back on and ride again in a few weeks- on his OWN bike, thankfully!

I'm blessed with great families- the one I was born into, the one I married into, and the one I nurture now.

A Mother's Wisdom

Friday morning I spent about an hour talking to my mom on the phone. She was on her front porch, reading in Philippians, and reflecting on 3:8- "I count all things as loss compared to the surpassing value of knowing Jesus Christ my Lord..." Often as mom talks, she can sound like she's preaching, and speaking almost poetically as she relates something close to her heart. Over the years, it's been easy for me and my brothers to simply smile and respond with, "Yeah, there goes Mom- getting all spiritual again!" But this time, I felt compelled to really listen to her. She spoke of her experiences in life, all that God has brought her through over the miles & years, and the things He has taught her and blessed her with. And yet, like the verse stated, she said she considered it all worthless in view of just knowing Christ as her Savior, Lord, and Friend.

Later in the morning, as I reflected on all she had shared, a couple of things began to occur to me. I suddenly realized, my mother is a sage- a woman of God with great wisdom and insight. The older I get, the more I want to learn from her, hear her life insights. I also began to understand how much like her I really am. Lisa pointed that out to me later in the day that, "You are so much like your mom- such a spiritual heart, seeing God in nature, loving beauty...You are definitely your momma's son!" I never thought of myself like that, but I'm actually honored by the comparison. She has such a heart for God and a deep fellowship with Him, I certainly hope to have a walk like that as I reach her years. She inspires me.

Separation Anxiety

I'm flying solo as a parent this week- Lisa left Saturday for an 8-day mission trip to Iquitos, Peru. She won't be back until next Saturday. Already, I feel her absence. Ansley went to work on Sat., Kelsey had plans with some friends, so I was left alone with my thoughts. I took a ride on my motorcycle, and felt a loneliness already setting in. Today, me and the girls just hung out after church, ate, watched a movie, and now that they are in bed, I feel the loneliness again. Funny, when you are around someone a lot, or even every night after work, you don't realize how much you rely on them until they are not around. When I'm away at work, or at a conference, camp, etc., I don't feel so separated from her; I know I can call her anytime. Yet now that she is so far away and so completely inaccessible in the jungles of Peru, I feel alone, fractured, incomplete without her close by. I understand a little more of what God talks about when He says of marriage, "The two shall become one flesh". I don't feel whole when Lisa is so far removed from me.

So I pray for her safety down there while she serves people in His name, and I pray for her safe return...

Dad & Daughter Road Trip

Friday I finished a 3-day road trip with my older daughter Ansley. We rode the motorcycle up in the mountains of North Carolina, riding on such famous roads as the Cherohala Skyway, the Blue Ridge Parkway, Scenic Highway 74, etc. We stayed at motorcycle campgrounds, and just filled our eyes and souls with the majesty and grandeur of the Smoky Mountains. We spent some time nosing through shops in Cherokee, visited the Wheels Through Time Museum in Maggie Valley, and mostly enjoyed some of the most beautiful roads and scenery in America.

Ansley completely soaked in the experience- she took pictures of everything, from massive clouds over high peaks, to small, colorful leaves we found on mountain trails. It enriched me watching her be so enriched by all we saw and did. She would say things like, "words can't describe this" or "pictures just can't capture this". She told me upon our return, "This was the best trip ever!" We both felt the presence of God up in those mountains, and felt a closeness to Him and to each other that I hope we carry with us for many years to come. I pray her heart will be always turned toward the Lord, the "Rock of our salvation", and we'll always take time to find refreshment in His mountains.

Riding North Alabama

I got back from my yearly road trip with my dad, and we had a great ride! We rode in east Alabama, with perfect weather each day. We first rode out to the famous Barber Vintage Motorsports Museum near Birmingham. It is 5 floors of close to 800 motorcycles and 75 race cars, from every corner of the globe. Walking in that place, was like entering the gates of biker heaven! I've never seen anything like it. We spent 5 hours in there, and could have went through it again. There were makes and models I had never heard of. I could have roamed those halls for another day. Amazing place.

We rode through the Talladega National Forest, on the Talladega Scenic Byway, which is beautiful. Not as high or as twisty as roads in NC, but a great ride anyway. While there, we rode other places as well, just enjoying the Alabama countryside. If I wasn't a Georgia boy at heart, I could make my home over there. Beautiful place.

Good to ride with my dad, for however many years we have left. I enjoy the time with him, not just on two wheels, but the talks, the laughs, the camaraderie of just being father & son. And more than that, the time we both spend, as sons of our Heavenly Father. All of this- priceless.

Our First Graduate

This past Saturday, Ansley graduated from high school. It's been an exciting, crazy, emotion-filled weekend. As we watched her walk forward, heard her name called, and she received her diploma, my mind went back 13 years to her first day of kindergarten. I recall taking her picture as she prepared to hop in the van with Lisa, and head off to her 1st day of school. I remember thinking about all the years ahead for her, and now I sat there, 13 years later, watching those years come to a close. A chapter of her life is closing, and a new one is about to be written. As it is for our family, as well. I sat there, watching her from afar, full of pride, nostalgia, and even a little sadness. She is preparing to enter college, young adulthood, and the wide world before her. She's not a little girl anymore...and yet, she'll always be my little girl. I sat there praying for her, wondering if we had done enough over the years, hoping she will remember all we had tried to instill in her life, and God reminded me, "She will. I gave her to you, you committed her back to Me as a child, and she's in My hands." Her future is bright- she is brilliant, beautiful, and motivated. And she is God's. I am grateful to be her earthly father. And she will always be my little girl.

Finishing Poorly

This past weekend I had a rather eye-opening experience, that greatly saddened me.
My brother Rick called me, asking about the last time I ever heard any news about our old youth pastor, from when we were teens (too many years ago..). "It's funny you asked," I said, "I was thinking about him just last week." Rick told me, "I think I found him."
Some background- Johnny (name changed) was an exciting, young, energetic youth pastor that came to our church when I was in 10th grade, and was a new believer. The youth group grew, reached many new kids for Christ, and Johnny was a role model for many of us. They were great years, and I made great memories in that youth group.
But Johnny had a character flaw, which became apparent after I graduated. He was found to have been committing adultery on his wife. He resigned his position, but they got counseling to preserve their marriage. They eventually moved back to Fla., to the church they came from, and he served under his former pastor again, who gave him another chance. We later heard he had another affair on his wife, which destroyed his marriage and his ministry. The last I had ever heard of Johnny, he was back up here in Ga., living in Conyers, running a successful sign-making business. It seemed, finally, all was settling down in his troubled life.
But Rick told me about a "MySpace" page he had found, with a

guy that looked remarkably like Johnny. The guy had tons of pics of himself at bars & nightclubs, surrounded by women much younger than him, with wild partying, drinking, etc. going on. He called himself a "celebrity photographer", and it looked like he made a living taking pictures of people living wildly & sinfully. He even had a couple of website links, which also seemed to include a nightclub DJ business, among other things.

I looked at him in all his pictures, and told Rick, "Yeah, that's him-I'd know his eyes and smile anywhere." Here he was, gray-haired, wrinkly, in his mid-50s, living like he was some godless 22 year old.

I was saddened and troubled by all I saw. This guy had once been such a great role model to so many of us when we were teens, and look where the choices in his life have brought him to. Sure, he may appear, may even believe, his life is one big party, but will he have anything to show for it, at life's end one day?

I pondered him much of the weekend, and thanked God my life hasn't gone the way of Johnny. At the end of life, all he will have in hand as he stands before God will be failed marriages, destroyed ministry, and a life wasted on vanity, sensuality, and selfish ambition. In other words, nothing.

I don't want that to ever be said of my life. I want to stand before my Father one day, and hear Him say, "Well done, son. Welcome home." In fact, if I could write my own epitaph for my tombstone, I hope it will be, "He walked with God, and brought others along." That's what I want my life characterized by. The things that will last.

Jesus said of the last days, "Sin will be rampant everywhere, and the love of many will grow cold. But the one who endures to the end will be saved." Matthew 24:12-13.

May I walk with God, bring others with me, and endure to the end.

Mini Cars & Super Moms

I'm reflecting on a wonderful Mother's Day weekend. Saturday, while Lisa and the girls left to meet my mom-in-law, sister-in-law, and nieces for lunch, I took off on my bike for my parents lake house, with two good friends of mine from high school, Pat & Karen Davis. We had an enjoyable ride to Oconee, with cool temps under cloudy skies. My parents had prepared a good old-fashioned Georgia fish fry for us, and we stuffed ourselves on fried catfish, croppy, and bass. We then all hopped on our bikes and rode, my parents leading the way down scenic country roads through horse and cattle country. We visited the MicroCar Museum in Madison, which was amazing! Over 300 mini-cars, all road-worthy, from all over the world.

Riding with my mom & dad, both nearly 70, I was humbled and grateful. Watching my mom holding onto my dad, helmet & Harley jacket, scarf waving in the breeze behind her, I found myself praying, "May my parents love life and love each other like this, for the rest of their days. And may Lisa and I share the same." I prayed that for Pat and Karen as well, riding with us all day.

Sunday was a blast as well! We celebrated what we called "SuperMom Sunday," inviting moms to participate in our morning children's worship hours with their children. They played the games, sang the songs, won door prizes, and shared in the Bible study times with their kids. I hope the moms all had fun, because we certainly enjoyed putting on the event for them!

That afternoon, my girls and I settled down for a time with Lisa, giving her our Mothers Day gifts and taking her out to dinner. Just an intimate afternoon and evening of showing her how much we deeply love and appreciate her.

As I read Proverbs 31:10-31, I think of Lisa, and both of our moms. All three of these precious women enrich my life in so many ways.

I couldn't have asked for a better mother to raise me to know, love and follow Christ. I couldn't have hoped for a better mom-in-law, who has poured herself into Lisa and loved me like her own son. And I couldn't have prayed for a better wife than Lisa, who fills up my senses and my heart with a love I feel so unworthy of but so grateful for, and who selflessly pours her life into our girls. She is truly an "excellent wife" of Proverbs 31, as are both our moms. And I pray my girls will grow up to follow in their footsteps.

MeMother & Maddey

It's been a hard day, at the end of a hard 6 days.

Lisa's grandmother, "MeMother" as we all called her, passed away last Friday. She was Lisa's last living grandparent, and they were close. She had been in declining health for several years, and had been in a nursing home in recent years. We got the call a week ago Monday, during my aforementioned vacation, that she had taken a turn for the worse, and might not make it through the week. It was a good thing we had not made any plans, as we got the call Friday morning of her passing. Even though it was expected, it was no easier when the news finally came. We spent the weekend going back and forth between Newnan and Dacula, for family times, the viewing, and I spoke at her funeral, delivering the eulogy while my old friend and mentor in ministry, Keith Moore, brought the message. In all, it was a beautiful memorial for a beautiful, godly woman, whom we who know Christ will see again. Keith called the service a "home-going celebration", and it was aptly named. "We do not grieve as those who have no hope...", as Paul wrote in 1 Thessalonians 4:13. Still, it was hard to say goodbye, and Lisa finally wept fully Sunday night back at our house, on the front porch at midnight.

Today, Maddey, our 13 year old Chihuahua, took a turn for the worse as well. Her health had declining over the past year, losing much of her eyesight, several of her teeth, and contracting canine diabetes, which compounded her health problems. We had been giving her insulin shots daily, but her health still deteriorated. She peed all the time, became unable to hold down food, and today we found her under our bed, breathing hard & heavy and unable to stand up.

It was time.

We took her to our local vet, who gently gave her the injection to put her down. She quietly and calmly died in our hands, kissing her head and stroking her back. It was a good death of a beloved family pet. It was especially hard on Lisa, not only because of MeMother's recent passing, but also because Maddey had been a gift from her to us, 13 years ago. Again, a difficult goodbye. We brought her body home and buried her down near the creek, where we buried Ivey, our first-ever dog, back in 2003.

God always seems to give His grace and loving presence in our sorrow, and I believe the Bible is clear that He is "near to the broken-hearted" Psalm 34:18. And so we allow ourselves to grieve, but we remember the gift of memories with those we love- and we look forward to the day when God will "make all things new", and the reunion will never end. No more goodbyes.

Anniversary & Antiques

Lisa & I celebrated 22 years of marriage this weekend! We spent Saturday roaming around the little town of Greensboro, GA, browsing the local antique shops & outdoor produce markets. We had a wonderful day, just the two of us, mingling with the locals & sampling the local cuisine. Greensboro is a great little town, kind of a miniature of Madison, GA.

We left there, and headed north to Watkinsville, where we stopped at a Ducati motorcycle dealership. Lisa of course humored me, and relaxed in the car while I nosed around all the bikes. Ah, she's a wonderful woman...

We made our way north to Bethlehem, GA, stopping in at another antique & specialty shop. Not really looking for anything in particular, as in Greensboro, just enjoying the day together. It felt like young love again, walking around these towns hand-in-hand, talking & laughing together. We finished the day on our front porch swing, with a pleasant breeze as the sun slowly set.

I can honestly say, my joy at being with her has not waned over the years, only grown. I love Lisa more today than when we started this journey together, and I hope to love her even more 22 years from now.

Atlantis

Last week my family & I enjoyed a once-in-a-lifetime week in the Bahamas, at the amazing Atlantis Resort on Paradise Island. This place is unlike anywhere I've ever been- all the buildings are designed to resemble what the "Lost Kingdom of Atlantis" might have looked like, at least in folklore. The place also boasts one of the largest array of aquariums in North America, definitely in the Caribbean. As you walk through the resort, you can pass through several aquariums, with overlooks, tunnels, tubes, etc. all passing through the giant tanks. There are over 50,000 fish between them all, with sharks, sting & manta rays, sawfish, barracuda, and countless others to be seen.

The resort also has a massive water park, AquaVentures, with the large Mayan Temple often seen on TV, which has slides passing through tubes in a giant shark tank. So many slides, tube rides, and "lazy rivers", one could spend every day just enjoying the water park.

What I enjoyed most were the times we actually spent in the ocean. The place is so vast, to get to one of their beaches, you need to be willing to walk for what seems like miles, or take a shuttle to one of the beachfront hotels then walk through to a beach. Can a resort be too big, when it's difficult to reach the beach??

We snorkeled several days offshore, and around some nearby shallow water reefs, and the abundance of underwater life was astounding! I never got tired of swimming around and just taking in all the amazing signs of life under the waves. I took a friend's underwater camera along, and snapped some great pictures above and below sea-level.

One of the highlights of the trip was a day we spent on Salt Cay, at a place called Blue Lagoon, where we spent several hours swimming with trained dolphins, observing sea lions, sea turtles, and snorkeling around in the bay chasing fish and catching crabs. I must say, swimming & playing with dolphins was an experience none of us will ever forget! These wonderful creatures are truly a tribute to the incredibly loving & creative God who designed & made them.

Another day, we took a bus ride to the southwest end of the island, and went out with Stuart Coves Excursions on a snorkeling trip. We dove on a coral reef, then a sunken airplane, and swam with sharks! The sharks were down about 30 ft below, but it was both thrilling and unnerving to be in the water with them. When some of them began to come to the surface, we all got out, and took lots of pics as the crew held a bait box near the surface to let us all get a good look at them. Large reef sharks, about 15 or so, all between 5-8 ft long. Unforgettable.

The trip was an experience my family (& my niece) will never forget. More than the incredible resort though, the beautiful islands, the incredible underwater life, and the wonderful people all made it most memorable for me. Our girls are getting older now, with Ansley 20 and moving out to UGA in August, and Kelsey beginning college herself next month as well. The memories we made together Lisa & I will cherish, and I hope the girls will too.

Christmas Spirit

I'm sitting here reflecting on this wonderful, memorable Christmas we just enjoyed. It's been a holiday I'll not soon forget. I enjoy the whole Christmas season, which for me begins on December 1, and runs until New Years day. And it's been quite a month- unseasonably cold for the deep South, lots of sickness going around, and I've been sick about half the month myself! In fact, I was pretty miserable in the two weeks leading up to Christmas Eve, with flu, sinus infection, and bronchitis symptoms all rolled together. Yuck. Then after a fever-filled night, I began to mend by the Eve, finally. It all left me pretty exhausted, in an already hectic, exhausting season.

Driving to the church early to help get ready for the Christmas Eve service, I was about to ask God, "I really need something to get me back in the Christmas spirit, Father," when He stopped my thoughts mid-sentence, speaking into my heart, "Its not about you, and working up some feeling. Its about My Son, and your worship of Him. Just choose to worship." I smiled, and I did, all the way there. I sang Christmas carols while driving, specifically "Come & worship, come & worship, worship Christ the newborn King" among others. And I worshipped all through the service, focusing on Christ, not looking for a feeling for me. But the feelings came anyway, in the form of a deep, satisfying joy.

This joy has sustained me all through the wonderful weekend! We joined up with some old friends out in Athens for a midnight candlelight service at their church, then home for Christmas with just the four of us. Christmas morning brought gift-unwrapping, Christmas music, smiles, laughter, and packing up for the trip to Christmas with Lisa's side of the family.

While down in Fayette with the Brown family, something happened that has not occurred in Georgia in about 119 years- snow on Christmas Day! It snowed all afternoon, on into the night, leaving 1-2 inches of white on everything. It was the most amazing sight for Christmas we had ever seen. Finally, all the "Winter Wonderland", "White Christmas" and other songs, we could sing down here in the heart of Georgia! Even today, there is still snow everywhere, two days after Christmas.

There's been a fair amount of adversity this Christmas, with my illness, then Ansley was sick, then we had issues with some gifts that didn't work right, a ticket while driving to Athens, to name a few. But really, these didn't affect the joy of Christmas, for me or my family members. We had plenty to laugh about, to enjoy, to worship and be thankful for. In the midst of the chaos and rush of the season, the heart of Christmas remains-

"God, who knows no before or after, entered time and space. God, who knows no boundaries, took on the shocking confines of a baby's skin, the ominous restraints of mortality... Little wonder a choir of angels broke out in spontaneous song, disturbing not only a few shepherds but the entire universe." –Philip Yancey, "The God I Never Knew", p.45.

God bless Christmas.

Snowed In

The new year has begun with a near-record winter blast. We have been snowed in since Sunday night. A huge winter front came through and dumped between 5-7 inches of snow on us beginning Sunday around 9:30pm, on through the next day. Its truly become a "winter wonderland"! Its been all the more enjoyable, given the fact that we had our first Christmas snow in over 100+ years, then just 3 weeks later we get another big snow. Roads were iced over, snow blanketed everything, schools & businesses were closed, and have been for 2 days now. In fact, now we have an arctic cold front coming down from the Midwest, and temps will dip into the teens during overnights. We could be stuck for another few days, since the roads will refreeze every night. The girls are out in Athens and Kennesaw respectively, so it's been Lisa, me, 4 dogs, and 2 snakes. And I've completely enjoyed my time with her. We've made a snowman (more like a snow blob), carved snow angels, had several snowball fights, attempted to sled our driveway (unsuccessfully), took a long hike out through snow-covered woods behind our property, and enjoyed watching our dogs play in the snow until they were shivering and soaked. Indoors, we did a lot of cleaning and a few home repairs, put on a roaring fire, got in a lot of good reading in a lot of good books, baked some cookies, watched some TV, and dipped in the hot tub. Been a great time, just my baby and me.

I've gotten a taste of what life will be like when we are officially "empty-nesters". Our girls are scarce when college is in session, and with the storm, its been just Lisa & me, all day, every day, neither being able to even get to work. And I can honestly say, I have not gotten tired of spending time with her. The past few days have been very special with her, and I have loved every minute together. Lisa is truly my wife, my love, my best friend.

More than even before, I know the years ahead for us will be joy-filled and intimate, as we grow old together.

Marriage is a love story set in a great war, ordained by God to be a picture of our life with Him, as John & Stasi Eldredge state in their new book, "Love & War". I'm all the more thankful to be journeying this life with Lisa, and a snowstorm has made me all the more convinced. God bless our road ahead.

The Hard Call

I had to do something Friday that only now am I able to sit down and write about. It has taken me the weekend to process it in my heart before God. Teddy, our Lhasa Apso dog for 8 years, has increasingly displayed bad habits that, the older he has gotten, the more impossible that have become to break. I've always heard Lhasas are wonderful, loving, loyal dogs, but very difficult to house train, esp. males. Well, Teddy has been largely untrainable all these years. He would always "do his business" outside on walks, but he always soiled around the house too, during the day when no one was home, or at night, when everyone was asleep. We had tried everything we could over the years to house-break him, to no avail. It got worse in recent years, with the other dogs we have taken in- Izzie & Johnnie, and Dexter. Teddy has fought Johnnie too often, bullied Dexter, impregnated Izzie before we could get her fixed, and stepped up his urine destruction of our home. We have replaced carpet around the house, replaced furniture & drapes, painted walls, etc. He has cost us literally thousands of dollars. And yet, he was the most affectionate, loyal little companion to me that I could ask for in a dog. He always wanted to be with me when I was home, always at my side. We had made the choice that at the right time, I would bring him to the vet, and we would "put him to sleep". Giving him away, or to the pound, or just abandon somewhere, were out of the question. We were the only family he had ever known. This was the most merciful thing to do. We just could not go another 8+ years with his worsening behavior. Friday, Feb. 18 was the day. Lisa did not want to be there, and we didn't want to involve the girls, prolonging the pain and stress for all of us. I would go it alone.

I took Teddy for one last walk down the driveway, something he always loved to do with me. He then enthusiastically jumped in my truck, ready to ride, not knowing where I was taking him. We arrived at the vet, and I took him inside to sign in. As we waited in the lobby, Teddy sat in my lap, shaking slightly, as the vet's office always made him nervous. A woman with an old, overweight golden retriever sat across from us, and he pulled at her leash, and came over to greet us. Teddy nervously growled at first, then as the friendly dog just sat down next to us and nosed Teddy, it's almost as if this old dog's warmth and presence comforted Teddy, and he stopped shaking. That dog sat next to us about the whole time, until they called us back. We were brought to one of the rooms, and waited for the vet to arrive. Teddy sat quietly on the table, with me stroking his fur. The vet finally entered, told me how they would proceed, and gave Teddy a sedative to put him to sleep, like before a surgery. When they left the room, I took Teddy, sat down in a chair, wrapped him up in my arms and stroked him, talking softly to him as he drifted off. He licked my hand several times, as if to say, "It's ok, I know you love me, and I love you too." Then he gently drifted off to sleep.

The vet came back in, asked if I wanted to stay or wait in the lobby while they administered the final phase, and I chose to exit and wait outside. About 10 minutes later, he called me back in, and I looked upon Teddy's now lifeless body, so full of life just minutes ago. It was a hard moment for me. They gave me a carry case to take him home in, and helped me to my truck. They are a wonderful team there- have treated all of our pets, and put Ivey & Maddie down for us as well.

I drove home, and found a spot down by the creek to bury Teddy, right next to Ivey & Maddie. After digging the hole, I held his body one last time, then laid him in and covered him up. With a heavy heart, I took a motorcycle ride, to clear my head and pour my heart out to God in my grief & growing guilt. The whole event raised anew the grief over Ivey's passing, so many years before. I realized how I still missed her, our very first dog. I rode, tears filling my eyes, and asked God to come into my grief & pain. I asked, as I had some years before, "Father, in the new Heaven and new earth, will you please give me Ivey, Maddie and Teddy again, perfected, never to lose them again? Or am I being childish?" Then Bible verses such as "He will wipe every tear from their eyes", and "Behold, I will make all things new", and "No eye has seen, no ear has heard, nor has it entered the thoughts of man, what God has in store for those who love Him", among others came to mind, and God asked me, "Would Heaven be all the sweeter to you if they were there?" To which I said, "Yes Father, definitely!" He replied, "Why would I not do this? Of course I will give them back to you." Tears of joy came flowing, and I almost had to pull over and stop. His comforting words filled my sad heart.

Do I believe animals have a soul, or there is some kind of animal heaven? Of course not. The Bible does not support those at all. Do I believe God will have animals of every kind, every time period there, for our pleasure and joy? Of course I do. If "the lion will lay down with the lamb", and if God promises joy unspeakable and pleasures beyond our wildest imaginations, then why not those people and things we have dearly and purely loved in this life? I believe every true joy, every simple pleasure, every pure love, is a picture and taste of Heaven, awaiting us. God gave us special animals to bond with in this life, and I see it within God's nature to give them to us in Heaven with Him, never to lose again. Even more so, those loved ones we have parted with, never to say goodbye to again as well.

"What do dogs do in Heaven?", John Eldredge once asked God after their dog Scout died. He heard God say, "They run." Run Teddy, run Maddie, run Ivey. I'll see you soon,

Dad's Heart

This has been a stressful week, in my immediate and extended family. My father had emergency triple bypass heart surgery this past Wednesday. He has been dealing with growing heart issues for several years now, with blood thinners for his arteries, three heart catheter procedures in the last two years, a stint put in one artery last summer. He has been experiencing chest pain and shortness of breath again since before Christmas, so my mother drove him to the VA hospital in Augusta, where his heart procedures have all been done before. They did blood tests, determined they needed to do another heart cath, then decided to send him to the hospital on nearby Ft. Gordon Army base. All this time, I and my brothers had been on the phone with Dad & Mom, keeping up with all that was going on. When they were informed that Dad would need a triple bypass, and it was scheduled for Thursday, I took off from work, packed a bag, and started for Augusta on Wednesday, so I could be with them that night and there as he left for surgery the next morning. Mark and Rick did the same, all arranging our schedules so we could be there.

While driving, I got a frantic phone call from my mom, sobbing heavily, unable to speak. I immediately thought the worst, that

Dad had a heart attack before the surgery, or had died suddenly. But she said, "As soon as we got here, they took him right away into surgery. They didn't want to wait until tomorrow." I said, "Mom, that's a good thing! They are doing this BEFORE he has a heart attack." It had just caught her off guard, and none of us were there yet to be with her. I assured her that all three of her boys would be there, within a few short hours.

I arrived early afternoon, Mark about an hour after me, and we picked Rick up at the airport by 5pm. All of Mom's boys were with her now. As we all waited and talked, the doctor came out and informed us the surgery went fantastic, they would be sewing him up and calling us back soon. Within another hour, we were all allowed back to see him. He was still out, with wires, tubes, IV's, etc. all attached to him. He looked worse than he was, they said. His heart was beating strong on its own, he would be coming to and breathing on his own before the night was over, and likely ready to eat and sit up by the next day.

We all spent the night at local hotel, enjoying some much-needed laughter and downtime. The next morning, Thursday, we were back at the hospital, and he was conversant, but only a little. We took turns sitting with him and talking with him, until the nurses wanted to get him up and moving. We all took a late lunch, roamed a local mall, and when we arrived back at 4pm, he looked like a new man! Sitting up, eating on his own, joking with the nurses and doctors. What a change in just a few hours! It was good seeing him looking better.

Mark and I had to leave Thursday night, but Rick would stay until Saturday. Every day, I've been calling several times, to talk to Mom, and now even Dad, out of ICU and in a private room. They say he will likely go home Monday, and that he is recovering like a man half his age. He's a tough old turkey, and he has taken good care of himself over the years- eating right, exercising, staying active and avoiding tobacco and alcohol abuse. Clean living has its benefits!

His mom, my Grandma Brooks, died of a heart attack at his age, 72, so Dad has beaten the odds. God is not through with him yet, as he and my mom touch many lives for Christ, everywhere they go. I'm not ready for him to go yet either- too much life left to live together, too many roads yet to ride together. And with this past him, and after what will be a painful recovery at times, the docs said his heart should be good for another 25+ years. I jokingly told him, "Your heart will outlast your mind now!" Not sure he thought that was funny.

Out of Control

It's been about a month now since my father's emergency heart surgery, and he has recovered remarkably. Off all pain medication, and mostly back to normal (he still has to be careful not to lift too much). We all are very happy with his progress. I look forward to some spring/summer/fall riding with him this year.

I'm also very proud of something he has recently accomplished, that he has never been known for. He wrote down an account of all he experienced during those days surrounding his surgery, things he thought and felt, words and Scripture God brought to him in the midst of the pain and uncertainty. My dad has never been much of a reader, much less a writer- I get those traits from my mother, a prolific reader and writer. But write he did, and below are some excerpts from his story, entitled "Out Of Control". "Being a typical man I've always felt I was, or should always be, in control of my life, and what I did would determine how things would go for me. Most men feel that they are in control, and when things get out of control it's a very disturbing feeling. So it was with me several months ago when I noticed increasing bouts of chest pain." Dad recounts the recurring problems, even though he had a heart stint installed three years prior. Thinking he could control it, he chose to wait until after the holidays to get checked out, writing, "Still thinking I was in control, this could have been a deadly mistake on my part."

He writes of being admitted, the emergency surgery being scheduled, and the feeling that everything was out of his hands- he no longer was in control. As my brothers and I rushed from all over to Augusta and be with our mother during the surgery, Dad recalls this- "I was handed a clipboard with paperwork for me to sign, giving them permission to operate. It was at this point things for me were 'Out Of Control'. I had signed my name and now had no control over what would happen to me." He recalled a verse from the Bible, Hebrews 13:5, which reads, "Never will I leave you, never will I forsake you." Dad writes, "I know now that in moments of great stress, though we may not be thinking of God, He is always thinking of us."

As previously written, the surgery went great, and though there have been pains, feelings of helplessness, exhaustion, Dad writes, "Reflecting back on all of this, my first question might be 'Where was God in all this?' I believe I know. When I was waiting too long to get help for my heart, He was holding back a heart attack, keeping my heart safe for surgery." He recites part of Philippians 4:7, "and the peace of God...will guard your hearts and minds in Christ Jesus." God was in total control, the whole time.

Dad concludes by stating, "I will not be in control anymore, I'm not very good at it. It could have cost me my life. I will leave control to God now and do my best to trust Him daily for direction."

"I have been young, and now am old, yet I have not seen the righteous forsaken or His descendants begging for bread."(Psalm

37:25)
Final footnote- the day my father had his heart surgery, my niece Rylee, Rick's daughter, prayed and gave her life to Christ back home in Dallas with Robyn her mother. Dad finishes with this- "He gave two people new hearts on Jan. 11, 2012. Mine as He rebuilt my heart physically, and spiritually as my granddaughter Rylee prayed with her mom to receive Christ in her heart that same day. God is good, God is faithful."
Yes He is.

Silver Anniversary

Yesterday marked the 25th anniversary of Lisa's & my wedding. It's hard to believe the years have flown by so quickly. In some ways, it seems like only yesterday to me. I remember the ceremony, the pride in my parent's eyes, the stunning beauty in a bridal gown walking down the aisle on her father's arm to me. Twenty five years...filled with laughter, joy, a few tears, lots of adventure, and most of all, God-given love. I wouldn't trade a day of it with her, and would do it all again, in a heartbeat.
Our families first met way back in 1972 or 73 I think, when my dad saw an ad in the local paper for a pickup truck for sale. We had recently moved to Fayetteville, Georgia from south Florida, and my dad wanted to get a pickup- that's what these Southerners drive, right? He bought that old, black Ford pickup from a guy named Milbur Brown- Lisa's father. Turns out, they lived a couple of houses up from friends of my parents, the Harvey's, who had also moved to Fayetteville from south Florida. We spent many a Saturday and/or Sunday at the Harvey's house, who had two girls and boy, all younger than me. I once met this kid from up the street named Tim, and I would go up and play at his house often, when my family visited the Harvey's. Tim had a little sister, Lisa,

with blond ponytails and an infectious smile. We never let her play "Army" or "Cowboys & Indians" with us.

As the years went by, my parents began to attend Flat Creek Baptist Church south of town, during my junior high and early high school years. It just so happened the Browns were members there, though Lisa was in grade school then junior high at the time. We later moved our membership to New Hope Baptist, closer to home, only to find the Browns had as well! Lisa and Tim were both active in the youth group. I never paid much attention to her then, me being the big high school upper classman by that time, Lisa the lowly junior high-er! That would soon change, though...

As a young college student, I served as a summer intern, camp counselor, and even Sunday School teacher at New Hope. One year at high school summer camp, I was assigned as a team leader of about 15 students, one of whom was- Lisa. As we got to know each again that week, she developed a "crush" on me, and I admittedly was attracted to her (not usually encouraged between campers and counselors!). She wanted to talk one evening after dinner, out on a swing by the cafeteria, and we talked about how she felt called to the ministry, as I had several years before. Hugh Kirby, the youth pastor at the time, later told me, "I was going to have a talk with you about getting too close to one of the campers, but God told me to stay out of it, He was up to something here."

We began to date after that, off and on during her last two years of high school. Proms, dances, football games, church activities- replaying it all again, with Lisa. The longer we were together, the more serious we became. I got to the point where I asked a friend from my high school years, Pam, how I would know if this was the "real thing" or not. She told me, "When you come to the point that you can't imagine life without her, and can't bear the thought

123

of her with anyone else, you'll know it's the real thing." I was there, and I knew it. My dad helped me find a diamond ring, I secretly got the approval of her father, and one night, on a swing set at a church (Lisa loved to swing), I asked this girl to marry me. She accepted, and we began to plan for our life together.

We were married on August 29, 1987, at New Hope Baptist, Keith Moore (my pastor and "big brother" in the Lord) officiating. Hugh sang, and family and friends celebrated with us. We moved several times over the years- lived in a little single-wide trailer in Fayetteville for a time, then our first little house in Lithonia when Ansley was born, a church-owned home in Snellville when Kelsey was born, two other houses in that town, before landing here, in Dacula. I've served churches in Peachtree City, Clarkston, Snellville, and now Dacula. Lisa has worked at several hospitals and a doctor's office. We've raised two lovely daughters, made a ton of memories, experienced many triumphs and a few tragedies along the way, but through it all, Lisa has been my soul mate, my lover, my best friend. Our love has done nothing but grow over the years, and I pray will continue to, as long as we both are alive. Its true- I can't imagine life with anyone else, would not have wanted to do life with anyone but Lisa. Aside from my relationship with Jesus Christ my Savior, the greatest love of my life is her. Happy 25th Anniversary, Lisa! (29 if you count our dating years)

May God see fit to bless us with at least 25 more, like both our parents.

8 AARON

*In May of 2012, I lost a dear friend to cancer. This is the account of our relationship, from my journals. It was a storied friendship, in my opinion.

Saturday, Sept. 27, 2008

Today I finished my vacation on the perfect day, in the perfect way. I reconnected and rode motorcycles with 3 more old high school friends, Pat & Karen Davis and Aaron Smith. We hadn't seen each other since graduating high school in 1981, and getting together was incredible. We met up at 9:30am, and rode north to Helen, stopping periodically to stretch, talk, and top off our gas tanks as needed. Gas has been scarce, so we had to get it where we found it. We ate at Hans Restaurant in Helen, sitting and talking, reminiscing, and laughing on into the afternoon. We nosed around a couple of bike shops in town, then hit the road again, riding great country roads around north Georgia before making our way back south. It was a fantastic day, with fantastic friends.

I arrived home after 8pm, tired but refreshed. I took a late night walk down the driveway, reflecting on my week... rode with my parents last weekend, rode with Jimmy & Lyle early this week, then with Pat, Karen, & Aaron today. All across the beautiful Georgia landscape. I gave thanks to God my Father, not only for all the blessings of the week, but for all the blessings of my life- my beloved wife & girls, my parents & brothers, my Hebron friends, my health, my walk with God. I heard Him speak into my heart, "It's My pleasure." A simple, common statement, but from God, it took on new meaning. The Bible says, "God delights to give good gifts to His children", and I know it's true. It brings God pleasure when we take pleasure in the life He gives us.

"I am, among men, most truly blessed..."

Sunday, May 2, 2010

Today was an exhausting but exhilarating day. I arrived at the church at about 7:45am, and began to get everything ready for a morning of RockiTown children's church hours. By 9:20 I hustled over to the main worship center to prepare to baptize a mom and her son who had recently come to Christ. It was an exciting moment, baptizing them together. I got back in time for the rest of our RockiTown worship times, and spoke both hours on "Be still, and know that I am God" (Psalm 46:10).

By 12:15pm, I was jumping in the car and racing around I-285 to arrive at First Baptist Atlanta and an afternoon baptism celebration for my old high school friend Aaron Smith. I have known Aaron since the 9th grade, and though the miles, the decades, and the circumstances of life have caused us to pass in and out of each other's lives, over the past couple of years we've begun talking more, and of course riding motorcycles together.

126

Then, back last fall, Aaron called me one Sunday afternoon, telling me he had trusted Christ at First Baptist Church of Atlanta! I was thrilled, to say the least. So when he asked me if I'd baptize him, I was honored. His mom was there, as well as Pat & Karen Davis, who have been friends with Aaron since high school as well, and several other family friends. It was a real privilege to help Aaron take this step in his new walk with Christ. I told Him, "We've been friends for many years, and now I'm thrilled to call you my brother as well."

After returning for a brief rest, I prepared for the evening worship service, which I was to preach in. I was excited for the opportunity, as in the 10+ years I've been at Hebron, I've only been given the chance to preach, outside of the children's ministry, on two occasions. I spoke on Courage- in our personal lives, our homes, in the world, for our children. My opening text was from 2 Timothy 1:7- "God has not given us a spirit of fear, but of power, love, and a sound mind." Several told me afterward that it was a message they needed to hear, and were encouraged by it. I related the courage of my friend Aaron, in boldly taking his stand for Christ.

In all, it was an exhausting, exhilarating day. I can't think of a better way to spend myself.

Sat, July 2, 2011

Friday morning I set out on a two-day moto-adventure with my old high school friend, Aaron Smith. We had planned this trip about a month prior, with Aaron wanting to ride some of the famous roads up in western North Carolina and east Tennessee that he had never ridden before. We would also tent camp up there, something I always enjoy. I was looking forward to the trip with him.

We met up at I-985 above the Mall of Ga at 9am Friday, and blasted all the way up to 441, and rode this beautiful road up into the mountains. We stopped off at Tallulah Gorge, a place he'd never been before. Deep canyon, looks to be a half-mile to the river below. We continued on into North Carolina, fueling the bikes and ourselves as needed. We decided to ride a route known as the "Smoking Dragon", which entails riding 441 through the Great Smoky Mountains National Park up to Gatlinburg, then west over to Cades Cove and Townsend. We then picked up the Foothills Scenic Parkway, and rode it south to 129 and the famous "Tail of the Dragon" section. None of which he had ever ridden before. The roads were not highly crowded, and we enjoyed beautiful views and exciting, curvy roads. In all, the "Smoking Dragon" loop was about 145+ miles, on top of what we had ridden to get there. We rode Hwy 28 over into Stecoah, to the Ironhorse Motorcycle Campground, and honestly, I've ridden the Dragon so many times, I enjoyed the ride on 28 over to Stecoah more than the Dragon, not nearly as twisty.

We arrived at Ironhorse around 5:30pm, checked in, made camp, and ate burgers with sweet potato fries they were serving. After a relaxing evening of a game of pool, time by a big campfire they started, and some good conversation, we turned in to our tents. I slept good, with the night sounds of crickets chirping, and the stream gurgling that we had camped by.

By morning, we were up, ate, showered, packed, and on the road by about 9:30am. We rode south to Robbinsville, gassed up, then rode over to the Cherohala Skyway, which he had never ridden either. I love this road, with its sky-high turns that skirt the tops of the mountains. The view of the Smokies is breathtaking, from nearly every overlook. We came upon a sport biker around a corner near the high point on the parkway, who had just slid out in a curve, and was picking up his bike. We quickly pulled over to help, when suddenly he hopped back on, fired it up, and took off. We looked at each other and I said, "I guess he was more embarrassed than hurt!" We followed the Cherohala into Tennessee, to Tellico Plains, and enjoyed a late lunch at the Tellicafe', popular with riders coming off the skyway. We then turned south on 68, turned onto 294 and rode through the Fields of the Wood, home to the world's largest display of the Ten Commandments. Again, Aaron had never seen this before. It evokes a definite "Wow" every time I'm there. We continued on back into NC, to 19/129 South, back into Georgia. Riding through Blairsville, we detoured over to Helen, which was ridiculously crowded with holiday weekend tourists. Couldn't get out of there fast enough. Riding on down to Cleveland, we parted company, he over to GA 400, me south to Gainesville and on to home. I pulled in about 6pm, tired, sore, stiff, sunburned, but satisfied. It was a good two-day ride.

Aaron has only been a Christian now for a couple of years, and spending the time riding, eating, hanging out, and camping together gave us plenty of time to talk, reflect, pray, and encourage each other. I hope it was as enjoyable and encouraging for him as it was for me. Motorcycling, mountains, a good friend, a still relatively new brother in the Lord. Time well-spent.

Wednesday, April 11, 2012

A very dear friend of mine is in the fight of his life right now. Aaron Smith, high school friend, motorcycle riding buddy, and as of three years ago, brother in Christ, is battling advanced prostate cancer, which has spread into his bones and lower spine. It tears me up to see and hear him struggle in agony and exhaustion. Aaron and I go way back, to our freshman year in high school, 1977. We met our first day of school. I had difficult junior high years, as many kids do, and my first day in high school was not starting well. I had no classes with my friends, and by 3rd period was hopelessly lost in the bowels of this huge new world called high school. Overwhelmed, I stood in the back corner of a bathroom, quietly sobbing, embarrassed to go any further. Suddenly, a blond-haired kid with braces and a 9th grade "bro-stache" walked in, looked at me and asked, "Dude, what's wrong?" I told him my dilemma; he looked at my schedule and replied, "Hey, you're in my class! C'mon, I'll take you there." No ridicule, no ignoring, he just offered help. His name was Aaron. He was the first friend I made in high school.

We stayed friends, but our lives took different paths toward the end of our school years. His parents divorced, and Aaron sank into many of the pitfalls that so many teens succumb to. I came to Christ by 11th grade, and got very involved in church. After our school days, Aaron joined the Air Force and found an aptitude for flying. He later became an airline pilot, living the "glamorous" jet-setting life for the next several decades. I went to college and seminary, got married, started a family, and pursued a calling of serving God in full-time ministry. Except occasionally at class reunions, we lost contact with each other.

Our paths crossed again almost 4 years ago, when through another old high school friend, Pat Davis, we reconnected on Facebook. The three of us began meeting up and going on motorcycle rides, and spent much time talking and catching up with each other's lives and experiences. They both knew I had become a Christian back in school and was a minister now, and we shared many conversations about spiritual things. The years and the miles apart had made all three of us very close once we reconnected.

One Sunday afternoon, I got a call from Aaron, who said with a wavering voice, "Rob, I have something to tell you. I've been going to Dr. Stanley's church, First Baptist Atlanta for the past month, and this morning I gave my life to Christ! I wanted you to be the first to know." Words can't describe the joy I felt, and I choked up with emotion. Within a couple of months, I had the privilege of baptizing Aaron, at FBCA, with his mom, sister, Pat & Karen, and other family and friends all present. In the years since then, I've seen Aaron grow in Christ dramatically, devouring God's Word, getting involved in ministry at his new church, and sharing his new-found faith in Christ with people at every opportunity. We have continued to take motorcycle road trips together, enjoying our renewed friendship and shared faith after all these years.

I got a call from him last month, beginning almost the same way one did over three years ago- "Rob, I have something to tell you..." What he told me this time made my heart stop. "I have prostate cancer. It's highly advanced, stage 4, and I'm scared." I was stunned. Not Aaron! The last few years flashed through my mind. We prayed together, shed some tears together, and I pledged, along with Pat, to do whatever possible for him as he goes through this fiery trial. After a battery of tests and scans, the cancer has been found in his bones as well, the pelvic region, in his lower spinal vertebrae, and now his liver. The outlook is bleak, the road long and torturous.

Aaron is considering his options, looking at various treatments and aggressive measures, even considering natural approaches such as macrobiotics. My aunt Judy is a 21-year stage 4 cancer survivor, and I've put them in contact with each other. God only knows where this will all go, what the outcome will be.

So I'm praying for my friend and my brother, asking God for his healing and wholeness. I'm reminded how fragile and short this life is, "like a vapor" as the Bible states. God has not promised us smooth sailing and clear skies in this life, but no matter what we face, He promises us His presence and grace. And whenever our end here is, those of us who know Him and have entrusted our lives to Him await the promise of the real life to come, never to struggle and suffer again. That is our great hope. That is Aaron's great hope. That is my great hope.

Pray for Aaron- my friend, my brother in Christ.

Wednesday, May 16, 2012

This morning, I got the call I hoped would not come. Aaron Smith, my close friend and brother in Christ, passed away in the early morning hours. His sister Elizabeth informed me. I was stunned, speechless. It all happened so fast, and I couldn't get my head around it. Over the past couple of months, this cancer moved so rapidly there was almost nothing that could be done to stop it, or even slow it down. Aaron had been admitted to Piedmont Hospital, where they began aggressive chemo treatments. I had been down there to see him numerous times, even spent the night to give the family a break. He fought bravely, but ultimately, the cancer overpowered modern medicine, and he was sent to a hospice down close to where we all grew up. There he died, not two days after being settled.

Over the past few months of his battle, we had many conversations. He went from fear to determination to urgency in sharing Christ with people, and finally to peace and resignation, that whatever happens, Christ would be glorified and many would come to faith as a result. One of the nights I was with him at Piedmont, about 2am after getting another overnight round of pain meds, he wanted to talk. We sat up until 3am, talking about the things he had been learning in Bible study recently, the opportunities God had given him to share Christ with visitors and hospital personnel, and his thoughts on where all this was going. He said, "Rob, I have to tell you something. I'm not afraid anymore. Whatever God's plan for me is, I'm at peace with it. If I get well, I'll keep living for Christ. If I don't, well, I'll be with Christ. I can't lose either way." I shared the verses in Philippians 1:20-24, where Paul states, "For to me, to live is Christ, and to die is gain." A win-win situation for a Christ follower.

I then felt led to share with him something God had spoken to me a couple of weeks earlier, but had been hesitant to share with anyone yet, in hopes Aaron would get well. I shared with him the passage in John 12:24, where Jesus declares, "unless a grain of wheat falls into the earth and dies, it remains by itself alone; but if it dies, it bears much fruit." At this Aaron began to weep heavily and loudly, grasped my hand, and said, "Rob, that's the exact thing I've been praying lately! That if by my death, they (several family and friends) come to faith in Christ, it will have been worth it all. I'm so happy, so happy." I was stunned. The very verse God had laid on my heart for Aaron, but didn't want anyone to know for fear they would think I was predicting his death, was the very verse he himself had been praying. Wow.

So here I sit, grieving the loss of my dear friend, but cherishing all the great memories we made together, and resolute that I will do my part to carry out that commission. I will share the life and love of Christ with those Aaron wanted to see saved, and with any others God gives opportunity. That will be the highest I can do to honor my friend, fulfill his desires. This seed will bear much fruit.

 I love you Aaron, my friend and my brother. And I'll see you again, one day.

Thursday, June 21, 2012

It's been more than a month since I last wrote anything here. After Aaron's death, I just couldn't bring myself to write anything for awhile, just wanted to leave up the last two posts about him. Since that time, I've had the privilege of speaking at his funeral, and assisting his family in sorting through his effects. At the funeral, I determined to tell his salvation story again, our years of renewed friendship and memories, and I challenged those present to confess their own need for Christ, and surrender their lives to Him. There are family members and dear friends of Aaron that I pray were impacted that day, and will come to Christ as he did. Aaron wanted that, more than anything else.

We completed another year of Vacation Bible Camp last week, "Boot Camp 2012" we called it. It was a military theme, and we saw over 1800 attend every day. 81 kids made decisions for Jesus Christ, that we know of, and we will be visiting families and baptizing new believers out of this extraordinary event for weeks and even months to come. I had the opportunity to do something super-fun, and it made a big hit with kids both times I did it- I rappelled out of the ceiling in full camo and gear, like an Army Ranger! I'm crazy, I know...

So now as we work through the rest of a busy summer, I'm reflecting on the loss of a friend, on gaining many new, young converts to Christ, and the impact our lives have on each other, and on God's Kingdom. I'm thankful to be able to do what I do, here at Hebron, at this stage in my life. Pointing people to Jesus, nudging them closer to a relationship with Him. Worth it all.

Oct. 3, 2012

The other day I was walking the dogs before going in to the office, praying for several friends and acquaintances I dearly want to come to Christ. Some I have been praying for over four years. I asked God, "I don't see anything happening. They seem to be as far from You as ever. Why?" I looked down, seeing acorns all over the ground underneath the huge oak tree in our front yard, and God spoke into my heart, saying, "These acorns don't sprout and take root immediately. It takes time to grow into a tree like this. There is more going on than you can see right now."

I realized God is at work in the lives of those I am praying for, in ways I don't even know. I happened to talk later that day with Elizabeth, the sister of my friend Aaron who went home to Heaven this past May. I told her what God had spoken to me, and she exclaimed, "Wow, that is incredible! What an answer to my prayers. I just spoke with Dad, and he told me he has starting to think he should find a good church. I also gave him a new Bible, and told him to start reading in John. He said he would. God is working on him!" Her dad has been one of those I have been praying for, since before Aaron died.

That evening, I got a call from a friend named Tom, whom I have been praying for as well. We had not talked since I sent him a lengthy, heart-felt Facebook message, entreating him to come to Christ. That was back in July, I think. He said he had been thinking about me lately, and wanted to get together and ride some this fall. I gave him some times I would be free to go, and he said he'd try to work out some of them. Again, God at work in Tom's life, keeping us connected so I have opportunities to share the love of Christ with another good friend.

So often, in our "instant everything" culture, we expect God to work the same way as our smart phones- instant input, instant response. But God works on a different timetable, in much deeper ways than we know. I'm reminded of this great verse in 2 Peter 3:9-

"The Lord is not slow in keeping his promise, as some understand slowness. He is patient with you, not wanting anyone to perish, but everyone to come to repentance."

When you can't see His hand at work, you can always trust His heart. He is working.

9 MISCELLANEA

Tough Getting Old

2008 hasn't started very healthy for me. Over the holidays, I had a bad head & chest cold for several days. I ate too much and have been trying to diet some and get back in shape, not very successfully. And now, over the past 2 weeks, I've developed some kind of intestinal infection, leaving me feeling lousy most days. On top of all that, for months I've been struggling with a pinched nerve between my shoulder blades, giving me a fair amount of neck & shoulder pain daily. Not a great start to a new year!

It definitely seems like the older I become, the easier it is to get sick or get injuries, yet its harder to get and stay in shape and harder to eat healthy enough to feel good. Entering middle age is a pain- literally & figuratively!

I've been reading a book about the life and writings of the late

Rich Mullins, whom I've written about before here. My all-time favorite musician, no doubt. In the final chapter of the book, the author shares many of Rich's thoughts on aging, death, and the life to come for followers of Christ. I was encouraged by a few lines from one of his old songs-

Live like you'll die tomorrow
Die knowing you'll live forever
Love like you'll leave tomorrow
Believing love lasts forever.

He also spoke these words-
"Remember that after we die...Christ is going to raise us up again, and somehow we'll be a body still. But we'll be different than we are now. A new body's what we get- and I've got a great one on order!"
"A little while after you're dead, you'll be rotted away anyway...It's not gonna matter if you had a few scars. It will matter if you didn't live."
I'm reminded of what Saint Paul wrote in 1 Corinthians 15:53-
"This perishable body must put on imperishability, and this mortal body must put on immortality."

So as tough as it is to get older, I have the confidence that when this body wears out, a new, improved model awaits me, with an eternal warranty. And that is when life will really begin...

Class Reunion

Over the weekend I had the opportunity to attend a high school class reunion/cookout, back in Fayetteville. It was actually a combination of classes, namely '81 (my year), '82 and '83. I rode down and met my life-long friend Lyle, and we drove out to the location together. It was a great night of seeing and catching up with old friends. I'm always amazed at the stories I hear, of the things that have happened in so many lives since our last reunion. Some are on their 2nd or even 3rd marriage, acting excited and hopeful for better days ahead. Some who married right out of high school, whom no one thought would ever make it, have actually defied the odds and stayed together and stayed in love across the years. That was a very encouraging thing to see. So many of us have kids that are now graduating, and we wonder, "Wow- are we really getting that old??" Some that I didn't know too well in school I've come to know better, like the captain of the cheerleading squad who along with raising 3 kids of her own, has adopted the 2 children of her drug addict brother. As she told me about it all, I saw the pain and sadness in her eyes, yet I marveled at the courage and determination she possessed, to raise and love those kids as her very own. I hugged her and said, "You are doing an amazing, honorable thing. God's going to bless you for that." So many stories in so many lives, it was really too short a time to spend with them all. Lyle and I just walked among them, listening to their stories and giving encouragement to these classmates we loved so much.

I left with a heavy heart, wishing I could spend so much more time with so many of them. These were the people I grew up with, and though we have gone our separate ways, we will always have a deep connection to each other. And if God can continue to use me to speak His love into their lives, I hope I'll always be ready and available. I look forward to the next time we are all together again.

Growing Young

I've been really feeling my age lately, and I don't like it. Since 2008 began, I've had one thing after another go wrong physically, it seems. Abdominal pains and sickness the first few months, neck and upper back problems that have caused fever headaches and migraines, physical therapy now for degenerative disks that have been discovered in my neck, and now I'm getting bronchitis! I just can't win.

I was hospital visiting last week, and on 2 different occasions patients told me, "You have teenage daughters? You don't look older than 24!" Although I was flattered by their compliments, I felt like saying, "Yeah? But I feel like 64."

Not only that, my motorcycle is over 10 years old, and has over 33k miles on it. Things are starting to break down with it as well- ignition switch went out, front fork is leaking (that's a big job), lights are not working right, all the fluids, filters, and plugs need replacing....I'm feeling a new kinship with this old bike.

God has used all this to remind me how fleeting & fragile things of this life are. Health is short-lived, and all things begin to break down over time. But it's good to know that God will make all things new for us one day. I'll get a new body- with "unlimited miles, unlimited warranty". The older I get, I more I place my hope in this promise-

"Therefore we do not lose heart. Though outwardly we are wasting away, yet inwardly we are being renewed day by day." 2 Corinthians 4:16

Rich Mullins called it, "Growing Young." That's what I want for my heart in Christ, even as the outward man eventually fails.

Peace

The other day in my morning prayer and reading time, I was

having difficulty staying focused- so much was swirling through my mind, weighing on my heart. The summer is here, all our big events are now staring me in the face- will we be ready? I've got a million things to do...

I thought of my girls- it seems we have so little time to talk these days, much less about spiritual things. I feel I have no spiritual influence with them anymore. Will they walk with God through high school and now college? Or will they walk away? I worry so often...

I set everything down, closed my eyes, and just prayed, "Father, what do You have for me today? What do I need to hear from You? What do I need from You?"

After a moment, He spoke very clearly into my heart:

"Peace"

"Yes Father, That's exactly what I need. Peace. I've had none lately. Teach me about Your peace, enable me to walk in Your peace."

The next morning, He wasn't through with me. I felt a leading to look up some Bible verses about peace, and soon found myself in Philippians 4:6-7,

"Be anxious for nothing, but in everything by prayer and petitions with thanksgiving make your requests known to God. And the peace of God, which passes all understanding, will guard your hearts and minds in Christ Jesus."

Wow- That is exactly what I've been needing. I spend my time worrying over things in my family, my work, my life, our world...I have not had peace. If I'll spend more time talking to God about it all, less time fretting, He will give an indescribable peace, which will guard my heart and mind.

Peace of mind & heart- I need it, only He can give it.

The Beach

Last week we got away for some much-needed rest after Vacation Bible Camp. We spent the week in Perdido Key, FL., soaking up the sun, swimming in the surf, and having fun with friends who came down with us. We hunted ghost crabs at night, collected shells and sea critters by day, and experienced a full moon over the ocean for several nights. So much beauty, so little time...
Each day, the surf conditions were different. One day, there would be clumps of seaweed full of tiny crabs, sea horses, and colorful fish; another day, the surf would be calm, and the floor full of hermit crabs, starfish & sand dollars. Every day was different, like an entirely different ocean. I would go for a run down the beach every night, by the light of the moon, with the sand cool & wet beneath my feet. I felt the warm presence of God in everything, from the tiniest creatures in the water, to the calm beauty of the moon reflecting over the waves.
I hear some say that they don't see God in anything of this world. I don't understand that. I see Him in everything around me. I guess if you are not looking for Him, or don't want to find Him, you won't. But if you turn your heart to Him, tune in to Him, you will find Him. He says, "If you seek Me, you will find Me, if you seek Me with all your heart." Jeremiah 29:13
Everywhere I go, Lord, I see You.

Looking at 45

I turned 45 today.
I remember when I was younger, and my parents were in their mid-forties. I thought they were sooo old! Now, it doesn't seem so bad to me. I still have all of my hair, it still has most of its color, I still have good health. In fact, I feel half my age...well, most of the time. Everyone says I look young, I dress young, and I act

young (I hope that's a good thing). I feel young, truth be known. My staff took me out to lunch today, and gave me funny cards about the benefits & troubles with aging, and we had a great time munching on chips at a Mex diner. Lisa & the girls fixed me dinner & dessert this evening, then gave me their gifts- a small home theater system for the basement, and a cool reclining couch. Sunday football, here I come!

Many friends & family called, emailed, or text-messaged their best wishes, and it was great hearing from everyone. It's been a pretty good day, considering I'm now 45.

The only thing that unnerves me about 45 is- its 5 short years to 50. Half a century old! 2003 was just 5 years ago, and it seems like yesterday. 50 will be here before I know it. That's sobering. Time marches on...

I know my days have been marked out for me, and my times are in His hands. So whether I have another 45 years, or just a few more, I want them to count- for Christ, and for those around me. And I wouldn't mind keeping my hair & health a little longer, as well...

Ragamuffin Gospel

I've been re-reading a book I recommended to a friend, a book called "The Ragamuffin Gospel" by Brennan Manning. I've actually read it 2x before, and every time I return to it, God speaks to me more, and points me deeper into His heart & His Word. Manning's main purpose is to expose the falsehoods we have fallen into as the modern church, namely that we no longer understand the grace & love of God, and have replaced these with a gospel of good works, personal discipline, and self-denial. He says, "The bending of the mind by the powers of this world has twisted the gospel of grace into religious bondage and distorted the image of God into an eternal, small-minded bookkeeper" going on to say "Too many Christians are living in the house of fear and not the house of grace."

Grace means we have been bought, paid for, and are wholly accepted by the One "who loved me and gave Himself for me." (Galatians 2:20)

Love means we are completely and passionately loved & pursued, without reservation and without condemnation, by the "furious love of God" as Chesterson called it. "He is the only God man has ever heard of who loves sinners," Manning writes.

I love his explanation of the true gospel of grace-

"This is the God of the gospel of grace: A God, who out of love for us, sent the only Son He ever had wrapped in our skin. He learned how to walk, stumbled and fell, cried for His milk, sweated blood in the night, was lashed with a whip and showered with spit, was fixed to a cross and died whispering forgiveness on us all..." then rose again to prove it.

Its less about doing, more about being. Not about us, all about Him.

Grazie Signore

I'm still reading Manning's "Ragamuffin Gospel", and God is using it and His Word to speak to me daily.

I just finished a chapter called, "Grazie, Signore", which means "Thank you, Lord". He begins with a touching story of a young woman who has had to undergo facial surgery to remove a tumor from her cheek. Her mouth is now slightly twisted, due to a tiny nerve that had to be severed to remove the tumor. As the doctor sadly explains the permanence of this side-effect to her, the husband stands by her side, gently stroking her hair & face. The doctor steps back, and watches in humble awe as the young man bends over his love, and whispers, "I like it. Its kind of cute." He then twists his own lips slightly to conform to hers, to show her that their kiss still works.

That story grips my heart for some reason. It almost moves me to tears every time I read it. That kind of love & compassion is truly beautiful, humbling, and of God. In fact, it is a picture of the love of God for us, displayed in Jesus Christ.

*"He who knew no sin **became sin for us**, that we might become the righteousness of God in Him."* 2 Corinthians 5:21

Manning concludes the chapter with a heart-felt prayer of praise, which I desire daily to make my own-

"Grazie Signore, for your lips twisted in love to accommodate my sinful self, for judging me not by my shabby good deeds but by your love that is your gift to me, for your unbearable forgiveness and infinite patience with me, for other people who have greater gifts than mine, and for the honesty to acknowledge that I am a ragamuffin. When the final curtain falls and you summon me home, may my last whispered word on earth be the wholehearted cry, 'Grazie Signore.'"

The Power of Forgiveness

I've come back to a story in the Gospels that grips my heart every time I read it. It is the story of the woman caught in adultery, found in John 8. Jesus is teaching in the Temple courtyard, with a large crowd gathered to hear Him. Suddenly, the Pharisees & other religious leaders burst through the crowd, dragging a woman caught in the act of adultery, and throw her down in front of Jesus & everyone. They boldly assert that Moses' law says they can stone her to death right on the spot, but ask Jesus, "What do you say?"

Now, as I try to imagine this whole scene, the shock and drama of

it become clear. Wherever & however they found this woman, they must have burst in on her and her lover, caught them in the act (which was a terrible sin, no doubt), dragged her out and down the street with probably little if anything on, kicking & screaming, all the while spitting on her, kicking & hitting her, taunting & verbally abusing her, all the way to the Temple. By the time they arrived with her, I imagine she was bloodied & dirty, sobbing uncontrollably, rightly fearing for her life. Then she was dumped unceremoniously at Jesus' feet.

With the crowd in shocked silence, the self-righteous Pharisees demanding an answer, Jesus mysteriously stooped & wrote in the dust. No one knows what He wrote, but He suddenly stood up, looked these men in the face, and demanded, "All right, but whichever one of you has had no sin in his own life, you throw the first stone!"

He then stooped to write in the dust again, the sobbing woman in a huddled heap beside Him. Whatever He wrote, coupled with what He had just said, one-by-one the accusers all turned to leave. Standing up, Jesus leaned over her and said, "Lady, where are your accusers?" Through her disheveled hair and sob-swollen eyes, she replied, "They're not here, Lord." And I imagine Jesus throwing a robe around her and helping her up as He said, "I don't accuse you either. But now go and leave your life of sin."

What an amazing scene this is! The cold cruelty of the religious leaders, who just wanted to use the occasion to try to trap Jesus in some way- contrasted with the uncompromising compassion of Jesus for this woman, is astounding to me. Many believe this woman was the same one who sometime later burst in on a dinner Jesus was attending, and anointed His head and feet with perfume, out of love and gratitude. Could this be Mary Magdalene, one of the most passionate and devoted followers of Jesus?

I know this- Jesus once said, "He who has been forgiven much loves much, and he who has been forgiven little loves little." May I always love much, realizing I have been loved and forgiven much.

May I always see people through the eyes of Jesus- not excusing their sin, but loving them with His love, which alone has the power to forgive and restore.

Focus

I've been feeling so distracted lately. I can't seem to stay concentrated on one thing for very long. My mind wanders to a dozen different things, constantly. I'll start reading something, only to get a phone call, overhear a conversation, remember something else I needed to do, etc. There are so many things grabbing for our attention these days- hundreds of channels on TV, in every room; music on the radio, on our mp3 players, on our computers, also our TV; cell phones with way more features than we need, constantly going off with calls or messages; more books & magazines than we can possible ever get to; endless surfing that can be done on the Internet, and so on. My attention span feels about as long as a 5 year old!

I recently joined a funny group on Facebook called, "I Have ADD And Wanted To Start A Group So That...Hey! Let's Go Ride Bikes!" for those of us easily distracted. Seemed an appropriate group to join! Does this come with age, have I been ingesting too much caffeine, am I trying to juggle too much in my life, or is something else at work? Maybe all of the above...

I have also felt disconnected spiritually lately, not as in tune with God's Spirit as I like to be. My prayer has become random and scatterbrained, and less frequent. I went for my nightly jog the other night, under the bright moon, and when I finished, I just sat down at the end of the driveway for a while, to try to talk to God some. I asked Him, "Father, what's wrong with me? What does my heart need from you?" Rather quickly, He spoke to my heart, "Focus." Yes, I certainly need that. I asked, "What do I do?" He said, "Stay with Me, linger here." I did linger there, for about another 30 minutes. Nothing majestic happened, the skies didn't open up and angels didn't sing, but I just sat in His presence, enjoyed the beautiful moon-lit night, and felt His presence and pleasure, like sitting in my dad's lap as a kid, just enjoying being outside together.

I need to "FOCUS"- be more intentional about my morning prayer and reading time with Him, and meet Him our here every night I can, to commune with Him. I want Him to again be "My One Thing" like Rich Mullins used to sing about. That way, He'll come back into focus in my life.

"Now this is eternal life: that they may know You, the only true God, and Jesus Christ whom You have sent." John 17:3

The Main Event

I just finished reading a column by Charles Lowery, a noted speaker and author, about "The Main Event" of Christmas. It was a timely article for me, as I've been thinking about these things myself lately, the closer we get to Christmas.

He tells a story about a young boy who wanted to see the circus that was coming to town, but his poor family couldn't afford the ticket price. His father had told the boy if he could earn half, the father would cover the other half. Over the next couple of weeks, the boy earned his half, and good to his word, the father spotted him the rest.

Elated, the boy purchased his ticket on opening day, then ran down to Main Street in time for the Circus Parade. He was mesmerized by the lions, elephants, acrobats, clowns, etc., as they all pranced down the street. As the last clown danced by, the boy handed him his ticket, then ran back home.

Later, when his dad came home, he asked, "You're home from the circus a lot earlier than I expected. How was it?" The boy excitedly described all the sights, sounds, smells- the whole thrilling spectacle. Then he told about giving his ticket to the last clown. The father sadly picked his son up, set him on his lap, and said, "Son, I have some bad news. Today, you missed the main event, the circus. You only saw the parade."

I think so many people rush around during this season, shopping, eating, attending Christmas parades and spectacles, some maybe even enthusiastically. Yet this is also the time of the year with the most cases of depression and suicide. People are missing the Main Event.

To me, I can see why people can get down this time of year. It seems pointless to do the same thing, year after year- rush, shop, eat, repeat. The same Santa stuff, the same parties, the same gifts, the same tv specials, etc.

What makes Christmas really Christmas is Christ! We commemorate and celebrate the coming of the Savior, the long-awaited hope of mankind, the One who has come to save us from sin, despair, and separation. Its not fairy tale or tradition. He is the Main Event, the reason for the season. Every year, I want to experience, not the fluff of the stuff of "the holidays", but the Christ of Christmas.

This Christmas, I don't want to miss Jesus.

Endurance

With all the rain we've had, there's been no break for motorcycle riding, so I've done a considerable amount of reading! I just finished one of the most amazing books I've read in years. Its called "Endurance: Shackleton's Incredible Voyage", by Alfred Lansing. First written in 1959, it recounts the unbelievable tale of survival of an Antarctic expedition that went bad. I was mesmerized from the first pages.

Lansing tells the story of polar explorer Ernest Shackleton, and his plan to cross the continent of Antarctica with a team on foot. Leaving England in August of 1914 aboard the ship "Endurance", they sailed for South Georgia Island down near the Antarctic Circle, headed from there for the Weddell Sea off the Antarctic coast. Bound for Vahsel Bay, they were to have put ashore to begin their overland journey. In January of 1915, after battling through thousands of miles of ever-increasing pack ice over six weeks, the Endurance became locked inside an island of solid ice. For ten months the ice-bound ship and crew of 27 drifted west then northwest before the ice finally crushed the ship and it had to be abandoned in October of 1916. Shackleton and his men then had to endure life on the ice floes for 2-3 months, hoping currents would move the pack ice close enough to land for safe crossing. That never happened. Surviving on limited rations and whatever arctic game they could catch, Shackleton and his men were ice-bound for almost seven months before the drift began to break up and they were forced to take to the 3 boats they had dragged free of the Endurance before she went down.

The men then endured a freezing, violent sea journey across some of the most dangerous waters on the planet, the Brasfield Straits, finally reaching the remote Elephant Island after five days. It was the first solid ground they had stood upon in 497 days. On this harse, barren, storm-blown island, Shackleton left 22 of his men, while he took 4 with him to journey to back to South Georgia Island, some 650 nautical miles away, back across the storm-tossed South Atlantic seas. Miraculously, they found the island

and after several near-death attempts, made shore after 15 days at sea. Exhausted, frost-bitten, weak with malnutrition and various ailments, they then proceeded to cross the previously uncrossed island over 36 hours to a whaling station on the other side. Finally, after several failed attempts, Shackleton himself returned to his men left on Elephant Island August 30 1916, bringing the rest of the crew safely home.

Incredible, beyond imagination- to have survived months on the ice, then so many miles on open seas, twice, then to have crossed a previously uncrossed island with little more than the tattered clothes on their backs, then to return for his men at Elephant Island, who themselves survived against insurmountable odds, - courage doesn't even come close to describing this. As British explorer Duncan Carse said in 1955 after making the first overland crossing of South Georgia Island since Shackleton did, wrote, "I do not know how they did it, except that they had to." What Shackleton and his men did defines heroism and determination. Surely, the name of their ill-fated ship described the men across their whole ordeal- Endurance.

I look at my momentary, and at times trivial, trials in a new way. When all else is stripped away, what we are left with comes out. May my life be one day defined by courage, determination, compassion, wisdom, and an unshakeable faith in my God, who will see me through any trial, as He did the men of the Endurance, nearly 100 years ago.

Winter Olympics

I love the Winter Olympics. Every four years, I can't wait to watch them. I actually enjoy the Winter Games way more than the Summer Games when they come around. I don't know why that is- I don't participate in any winter sports myself. I don't ice skate, never played hockey, I'm a lousy skier, and a nominal snowboarder at best. But there is something about the winter Olympics every four years that just capture my attention & imagination. They are almost magical, mythic, to me. The snow-covered, mountainous locations, the exotic places like Lillehammer, Nagano, Torino, and Vancouver, the other-worldly beauty of each country's opening & closing ceremonies...they all just enchant me.

And of course, there are the heroes of each Games. I remember the Austrian, Franz Klammer, rocketing down the mountain in the 1976 Olympics. I became a fan of downhill skiing watching him. And the unlikely champions of the 1980 Games, the US hockey team, and their staggering win over the undefeated Soviets. What a moment. I remember watching Olaf "The Boss" Koss defeat the "Flying Dutchmen" to win gold in speed skating at Lillehammer, I think. I've never been a fan of men's figure skating, but watching Scott Hamilton do back flips on the ice, and win several golds in 1984, was amazing. And of course, the first time I ever saw this little American guy with long hair and a bandanna, Apolo Ohno, win gold in Torino, I became a fan of short track speed skating. I could go on- so many heroes, so many, many memories.

These Olympics have not disappointed either! Bode Miller medaling 3x, Lindsey Vonn & Julia Mancuso medaling several times each, all three in downhill, etc., has been spell-binding. Every time Apolo races, I'm on the edge of my seat, cheering him on now with 8 medals! And in the ski jump, witnessing Simon Amman jump 145 meters, he looked like he was going to land in the parking lot! Amazing. Then Steve Holcomb and his team win the first USA gold in bobsled in 62 years. But nothing can top watching Shaun White win the gold with super-human stunts and height in the snowboard half pipe, then with the gold already his, doing one last run that included a trick no one had ever attempted before, much less landed, was nothing short of fantastic. Even watching the couples' ice dancing (again, not one of my faves), and to see the young Canadians win all-around gold- their pure joy, the crowd's hysteria, was a proud moment not only for Canada, but we were cheering them, as well. Although I had hoped for a USA win in men's hockey, esp. on the 30-year anniversary of the "Miracle on Ice", I'm proud for Canada to have won on home ice, in the sport they invented. Even the closing ceremonies were moving and thrilling. Greatest Olympics I've ever watched.

Ah, I love the Winter Olympics. There's something about them that touch me deeply- the thrills, the chills, the splendor, the unity, the beauty. Maybe they remind me of an adventure we were created for, a unity and beauty that awaits us, and a triumph & celebration we will share one day ourselves, with our Creator, Savior, and Lover, our Lord.

"No eye has seen, no ear has heard, nor has it even entered the mind of man, what God has prepared for those who love Him..." 1 Corinthians 2:9

The Real Grand Design

British physicist Stephen Hawking is getting all kinds of press these days for statements in his latest book, "The Grand Design", asserting that no God created the world, its systems, or the universe. One article uses phrases such as "God did not create the universe, and the 'Big Bang' was an inevitable consequence of the laws of physics" and "God no longer has any place in theories on the creation of the universe due to a series of developments."

What developments, one might ask. The book apparently recounts "a series of theories that made a creator of the universe redundant." Hawking is quoted from the book as stating, "Because there is such a law as gravity, the universe can and will create itself from nothing. Spontaneous creation is the reason there is something rather than nothing, why the universe exists, why we exist."

Think about his statements for a moment- even the wording and language he uses are contradictory. Let's start with a definition of the word, "theory." Simply put, a theory is someone's ideas and assumptions on something, based on their interpretation of existing evidence. The theory of evolution is a way to attempt to explain the universe apart from God. So, those are the "series of developments- "a series of theories", i.e. ideas, assumptions??

Next, Hawking calls upon the law of gravity to prove "spontaneous creation." Any law, to even come into being, has to be created by an outside source/force. Adding that the universe can and will create itself out of nothing- how ridiculous is that?? How could the universe create itself, if it didn't exist? Crazy reasoning here. Bottom line: nothing + nothing= nothing. Always has, always will. There is no way for nothing to create something, to create itself. That's lunatic science at its best...or should I say, worst.

Hawking again is quoted as saying, "that makes the coincidences of our planetary conditions- the single sun, the lucky combination of Earth-sun distance and solar mass, far less remarkable, and far less compelling that the Earth was carefully designed just to please us human beings." Note his use of "coincidences" and "lucky." Is that what he thinks created the infinite complexity of everything in the universe? Coincidence and luck?? Wow- how scientific of him. To me, it takes far more faith to believe that "gazillions" of accidents, "lucky breaks" and chance occurrences over billions and billions of years created all we see and know, than to simply accept, "In the beginning, God created the heavens and the Earth." (Genesis 1:1)

Like all evolutionary theory, that's all Hawking's not-so-humble and inaccurate opinion. He's saying nothing new, nothing any different than every other atheist-evolutionist has been trying to assert for years. Creationist Ken Ham has often said that we all look at the world and universe around us through the filter of our belief system. So true. If one believes, as Hawking does, that God does not exist, then they will interpret all the evidence they see through that lens. If however, one begins with God, or at least is open to the existence of and creation by God, then the evidence will clearly point to Him. Hawking sees all the infinite complexity of the universe and says, "random chance." I look at the same evidence and conclude, "Divine Design."

My old friend Billy Britt once said, "You'll find what you're looking for," meaning, if you don't want to find God, you won't, plain and simple. You'll come to whatever conclusions you want to come to. But if you do want to find Him, you indeed will. Even God has said, "If you seek Me you will find Me, if you seek Me with all your heart." (Jeremiah 29:13)

Hawking and many others in science, education, news media, politics, and entertainment, all assert it is foolish to believe in God. But God says of them, "Only a fool says in his heart, 'there is no God.'" (Psalm 14:1) Let God's Word be true, and every man a liar...

Mineshaft Rescue

I was captivated by the dramatic rescue of the 33 Chilean miners, who had been trapped 1/2 mile below the surface in a collapsed mine. History unfolded before our eyes, moment by moment, on the TV screen. Amazing- these men had been trapped for 69 days, and every one of them survived. For the first 2 weeks, no one was even sure if they were alive, having no contact with the outside world. When communication was established, they were found alive, organized to survive, and in good cheer. Companies, governments, and individuals from around the globe rallied to aid Chile in reaching and recovering their men.

With the 1/2 mile shaft drilled, and the specially designed capsule in place to bring them up one by one, I was enthralled with the anticipation, the excitement, and the unbridled joy as cameras below and above captured each man's return to the surface. Upon stepping out, each man was greeted with cheers, chants, song, clapping, hugs, and kisses. It was glorious. Many dropped to their knees and prayed, holding Bibles, giving thanks to God before anything or anyone else. It never got old, watching each man's rescue and the joyous response from everyone.

What struck me as I watched was how similar the whole scene was to what is found in Scripture. First of all, the joy people expressed is a picture of the joy in Heaven when "one sinner repents" and comes to Christ (Luke 15:7). All of Heaven cheers and celebrates when a soul is saved, and brought into family of God. Amazing. Second, in the same way that those above could watch the men below via cameras that had been sent down, the Bible teaches that we are "surrounded by such a great cloud of witnesses" in Heaven (Hebrews 12:1). They are cheering us on, from the halls of Heaven! That can either bring an "Amen!" or "Oh me...", depending on how one is living. Third, the rescue images speak to me of what awaits Christ followers when we leave the confines of this earth, "ascend the shaft" to our real home, Heaven, and breathe the free air of eternity. The sheer joy and exhilaration of the miner's rescue is a little hint, a picture of the grand celebration that awaits us when we each arrive home ourselves. "No eye has seen, no ear has heard, no mind has conceived, what God has in store for His children." (1 Corinthians 2:9) The hugs, the kisses, the cheers and chants, the singing and celebrating, will be unlike anything we've ever known or seen. And we will party for all eternity, with the Creator, Lover, and Rescuer of our souls.

I am filled with anticipation.

Benji

I recently found an old Dr. James Dobson book on our shelves that I had never read, so I decided to open it. It is a collection of stories from Dobson's life, or folks he has known over the years. I found one in particular that gripped my heart, and have been sharing it since at every opportunity.

Dr. Dobson recounts how much his father was always a dog-lover, and enjoyed a special friendship with a toy terrier named Penny for 17 years. When Penny's health failed and they had to put him down, Dobson Sr. grieved for nine years, refusing to replace his little companion. Finally, he opened his heart to the possibility of another little toy terrier, but for months had no luck in finding one. Finally, answering an ad in the paper, Dobson Sr. and his wife drove across town to see the pup at a pet store. With a strict set of parameters in mind (pedigree papers, good temperament, six weeks old, all shots, etc.), they instead found the pup to be nine months old, no papers, in poor health, malnourished, and traumatized in a filthy, over-crowded kennel. Astonished that anyone would offer an animal in this condition, Dobson Sr. tells of the encounter with the pitiful little pup-

"He followed me about the room, meekly, his tiny tail clamped tightly down, a picture of dejection...He seemed to be saying, 'You look like a nice man, but I know you will be like all the rest.'..he put out his warm pink tongue and licked my hand, as if to say, 'Thanks anyway, for coming to see me.' They drove off, but suddenly turned around, not able to leave that little pup in there. Bringing the pitiful animal home, the Dobsons bathed him, got him all the proper medical attention, and put him on a healthy diet coupled with heaping helpings of TLC. Benji, has they named him, became a wonderful little addition to the family. As Dobson Sr. writes- "He thinks I am God Almighty when he comes to meet me in the morning, twisting and wiggling like he will tear himself in two. It is as though he will never allow himself to forget his private hell in the pet shop!"

I found this story to be a beautiful picture of why God Himself came into this world over 2000 years ago. I found this Bible verse, that really relates well to the above story-

"When the fullness of time had come, God sent forth His Son, born of a woman, born under the law, that He might redeem those under the law, that we might receive the adoption as sons." Galatians 4:4

The word "redeem" meant to "buy out of the market", specifically a slave market or an animal market. And everyone knows what "adoption" means. Together, these words tell us that God came for us, "entered the door" of this world, bought us with the precious blood of His Son Jesus, and adopted us as His very own. Dobson Sr. is a picture of God in the above story, except of course God came for us, fully knowing our condition, and in compassion reached out to us. We are "Benji" in the story, except of course that we have a choice- we can gladly receive our adoption as Benji did his, or we can say, "No thanks, I like it here in the 'pet shop.'" This Christmas, every time I see a Nativity, I want to remember Benji's adoption, and rejoice in my own. And may my response to my Master be the same as Benji's response to his master- brash, unhindered, whole-hearted worship.

Undying Lands

This morning I was thumbing through our bookshelves, and pulled out the copy I have of The Lord of the Rings: The Return of the King. I hadn't read it in years, and it's been a few years since I watched the movie trilogy. So I sat down and skipped around through the book. I remembered why I loved this particular part of the trilogy best, as well as the movie. Such beautiful, powerful images that evoke the message of the Gospels and Revelation. I particularly read the closing chapter, when Frodo joins Gandalf and the Elves on the journey out of the Grey Havens, leaving the shores of Middle Earth at last, to sail to the Undying Lands. It's a sad chapter of goodbyes, but then Tolkien gives a description of the first glimpses of their destination:
"Frodo smelled a sweet fragrance on the air and heard the sound of singing that came over the water... the grey rain-curtain turned all to silver glass and was rolled back, and he beheld white shores and beyond them a far green country under a swift sunrise."
I am reminded of the Scripture that promises, "No eye has seen, no ear has heard, and no mind has imagined what God has prepared for those who love Him." (1 Corinthians 2:9) We can't come close to imagining the wonder of the splendor we will behold when the "grey rain-curtain" of this life is pulled back, and we arrive at our true home, the undiscovered country, the Heaven being prepared for us. Our "Undying Lands".
I read one of the sections at the end of the Tolkien book, in

Appendix A, entitled "Here Follows a Part of the Tale of Aragorn and Arwen". Tolkien adds more detail to this romance that runs throughout all three books, and honestly, a separate movie could have been done on this tale alone! Without revealing every detail of this beautiful section, he recounts the early years of their love, their years apart, their reuniting and marriage, and their many years together. Yet Aragorn, being a mortal man, comes to the end of his days, and prepares to say goodbye to Arwen, eternal elf. As he chooses to lay down his life and breathe his last on his deathbed, even in Arwen's grief, she witnesses something amazing:

"...as he took her hand and kissed it, he fell into sleep. Then a great beauty was revealed in him, so that all who after came there looked on him in wonder; for they saw that the grace of his youth, and the valour of his manhood, and the wisdom and majesty of his age were blended together...an image of the splendour of the Kings of Men in glory undimmed before the breaking of the world."

This description struck me like a thunderclap, as I realized what Tolkien was painting a picture of. This is the splendor that awaits each of us who love and follow Christ, at the end of our days on this earth. Just like a great glory awaits us on the other shore, a great glory will be revealed IN us as well- "I consider that our present sufferings are not worthy to be compared with the glory that is to be revealed in us." (Romans 8:18) I so often don't feel like there is much glory in me to be revealed one day. I'm so often hobbled by sins, weaknesses, shortcomings. Yet God says, "Not only am I preparing an amazing place for you, I'm preparing an amazing new you, your true identity." I look forward to that day, before the new Heavens and new earth, made new with all the saints of the ages, forever.

That puts a spring in my step, as I walk this stuff of earth.

"Beloved, now are we the sons of God, and it doth not yet appear what we shall be: but we know that, when He shall appear, we shall be like Him; for we shall see Him just as He is." 1 John 3:2

10 THE ROAD GOES EVER ON

The Road goes ever on and on

Down from the door where it began.

Now far ahead the Road has gone,

And I must follow, if I can,

Pursuing it with eager feet,

Until it joins some larger way

Where many paths and errands meet.

And whither then? I cannot say. -JRR Tolkien

A friend once told me, "Life is like a road trip. Even if you know your final destination, the joy is still in the journey." I completely agree. The unexpected twists, turns, detours, discoveries, even the disappointments and setbacks- they all contribute to the great adventure. I haven't ridden as much as some, ridden more than others, but every mile so far has made a memory, has been a blessing. God's been good to me, more than I've deserved. I can only hope that I have been an encouragement to those I've met along the roads, as much as they have been to me. Even now every new person I meet leaves a piece of his/her story with me, and I'm enriched. Motorcycling and ministry have brought me that, and I pray will continue to.

I'm entering my second century this year, as well as embarking on a new career path, and the miles and years have left great impressions on my mind and heart. If life and riding has taught me anything, I think these might qualify as a few road-worthy lessons:

Embrace Life

All too often, I can get myopic in my view of the world, can get overly worried and stressed about things I frankly have no control over. Watching the news can be discouraging at best, infuriating at worst. Adversity strikes, often at the most inopportune times, sucker punching us and piercing our hearts with discouragement and despair. I'm aging, and no amount of treatments, diets, and exercise fads will change that. Life is unfair and even cruel at times, outside my front door. But despite all of this, I refuse to lament, refuse to curl up on the couch, refuse to spend my time griping and complaining. God has given me this one life to live down here, and I intend to live it to the full, enjoy it to the max, and follow His leading, wherever the road may take me. I once read this quote on a website, not sure who first penned it: "Life isn't measured by how many breaths you take, but rather by how many times life takes your breath away." There's a big, beautiful world outside my front door, and I want to breathe it all in, every day, until I draw my last breath. Jesus Himself once stated, "A thief comes to steal, kill and destroy. But I have come that they might have life, and have it to the full."(John 10:10) Sounds like an invitation to adventure, if you ask me.

Be Open to People

It's easy to become cynical about the human race, about human nature. And frankly, apart from God, mankind sure lends credibility to the theory of evolution at times. The stupidity, the ignorance, the brutality, the selfishness…despite our achievements in knowledge, technology, and prosperity, humankind can still be downright deleterious.

And yet, there is much good in our kind, much benevolence still in our nature, even in our fallen state. We really are more than the product of random, thoughtless, evolutionary processes, and that is never more evident than when someone shows compassion to his fellow man (and woman). Out on the road, I have seen the inherent goodness still within us, on display whenever people selflessly lend a hand to someone in need. We are creatures made in the image of our God, and though there are far too many times we do not reflect Him, there are plenty of times that we do. As evidenced within these pages, I have had the honor of being on both the giving and receiving end of good will, many times over. Like my riding buddy Mike once said before our big road trip, "The best part will be the people we'll meet." And it always has been.

Take That Trip

A guy I know has been talking for several years about doing a "coast-to-coast" ride, starting in Savannah, Georgia and running cross-country to Laguna Beach, California. Toes in the sand, both coasts. He's got it all planned out in his head, how much time it will take, stops along the way, photo ops, etc. And yet, every year he keeps backing down, citing one reason or another for not going. Frankly, I'm tired of hearing him talk about it. Excuses, excuses. I told him recently, "You're not getting any younger, bro. Take the time, take that trip." I think he is where we all so often get stuck. We hold big dreams, high hopes, grand ideas, and yet, when faced with the opportunity to take the plunge, we too often shrink back. I think it's a fear of failure, fear of the unknown, fear we don't have the time, that we have too many obligations to attend to. But no one ever arrived at the end of their life breathing a sigh of relief while declaring, "I played it safe, took no chances." God has given us one go-round on this earth, and I think He means for us to seize the opportunities presented to us. Whether it's that neighbor who could use a friend, that coworker who could use a hand, that person on the street who could use some compassion, as well as the career changes, the road trips, maybe we all should "take the time, take that trip." Colossians 4:5 says in part, "make the most of every opportunity." Good advice, for everything worthy of effort. I once saw this on a rider's t-shirt: "My life is not a journey to the grave with the intention of arriving safely in a pretty and well-preserved body, but rather I want to skid in broadside, thoroughly used up, totally worn out, loudly proclaiming, 'WOW...What a Ride!!'" So, I've decided to take that "coast-to-coast" with my friend Lyle, since we both are hitting the big 5-0 this summer, if "guy" won't do it. We'll tell him all about it when we get back. What's your "coast-to-coast"? What dream has God put in your heart that you need to act on? You're not getting any younger. Take the time, take that trip. You won't regret it.

Follow the Ultimate Road Captain

I often feel like I'm navigating life as through a fog. It's hard to see the way forward at times. Sudden changes strike us broadside, events we never saw coming. We don't know which way to turn, and we can't see what's ahead. It's an unnerving place, not feeling in control. And yet, if we will seek Him, God wants to be our "road captain", our way through the darkness, our light through the fog.

Recently I had a rather extraordinary dream. I was suddenly a child again, 8 or 9 years old, and I was on a school bus, about the third row back on the right, with my "Hot Wheels" tin lunch box (I really had one) and my Miami Dolphins book satchel (I had one of those too). Suddenly, the bus driver pulled the bus over to the curb, in a completely deserted, unfamiliar place. He got up, came to me, took me by the arm, and escorted me off the bus, firmly shoving me though the door. As I stood on the curb, watching the bus drive away, I felt a stab of fear, wondering, "Why did he do that to me? What do I do now?" Suddenly, I felt a great presence behind me, a large, strong, warm hand took my left hand, and a deep yet comforting voice spoke, "It's going to be okay. I got you. Let's go." I looked up, seeing no face in particular, but a large, reassuring father figure guiding me forward, holding my hand. The terror faded, replaced with a peace, and I thought, "I'm going to be fine."

I was reminded of these passages from the Bible-

"For I know the plans I have for you," declares the Lord, "plans to prosper you and not to harm you; plans to give you a future and a hope." Jeremiah 29:11

Trust in the Lord with all your heart, and do not lean on your own understanding. In all your ways acknowledge Him, and He will direct your paths. Proverbs 3:5-6

I take great comfort in these and many other verses I have read or others have sent me over the years. God is good, His ways perfect, His timing spot-on, His love for us unfailing. He proved it all by sending His Son Jesus Christ to pay the penalty for our sin, to restore us to His Father. Place your faith in Him, confess your sin to Him, and surrender control of your life to Him. Trust me, the Road Captain knows what He is doing. He knows the way to life.

There are more roads to ride, more miles to cover, more people to meet, more memories to make. With God as my guide, I know whatever happens on the road of life, He's got me. I'll be fine.

"And the road goes ever on and on..."

ABOUT THE AUTHOR

Rob describes himself as a "preacher, writer, and rider." He has served in vocational ministry since 1988, but is currently a church planter/pastor, a contributor to several motorcycle and ministry magazines, and a conference speaker. When Rob is not riding motorcycles, he enjoys wrenching on and buying/selling them. Rob lives in Dacula, Georgia with his beloved wife, daughters, and menagerie of pets.

www.rtbrooks.wordpress.com

www.misterrob.blogspot.com

Made in the USA
Lexington, KY
17 May 2014